The FIDDLE MUSIC of SCOTLAND

The cover illustration is of the famous Scots fiddler Niel Gow (1727-1807) from the portrait by Sir Henry Raeburn
in the Scottish National Portrait Gallery.

The FIDDLE MUSIC of SCOTLAND

· JAMES HUNTER ·

EDITED BY
ALASTAIR HARDIE and WILLIAM HARDIE

A COMPREHENSIVE ANNOTATED COLLECTION
OF 365 TUNES WITH A HISTORICAL INTRODUCTION

FOREWORD BY
· YEHUDI MENUHIN ·

The Hardie Press

ACKNOWLEDGEMENTS

I would like to thank the following publishers for their kind permission to include copyright works in this collection:

James S Kerr, Music Publishers, for Nos. 72, 263, 282, 291, 350, 351.
Shetland Music, for Nos. 218, 231.
J D C Publications Ltd., for No. 7.
Tonecolor Ltd., for No. 12.
Palace Music Company Ltd., for No. 17.
Panache Music Ltd., for No. 348.

In addition I would like to express my sincere gratitude to the many living composers who have given me permission to include their copyright compositions; to the executors of the late Willie MacPherson, Gideon Stove and J. Murdoch Henderson for permission to reproduce works by these composers; to Bill Hardie, Arthur Robertson, Angus Cameron and Douglas Lawrence for their kindness in notating their individual bowing instructions for particular tunes; to Peterhead Arbuthnot Museum for the use of an original manuscript. Special thanks are due to Bill Hardie for advice on bowing technique. I would also like to record my appreciation of the work done by Harvey Mitchell, without whose help and encouragement this book would not have come to fruition.

James Hunter

The Publisher acknowledges subsidy from
The Scottish Arts Council towards the
publication of this volume.

ISBN 0 946868 03 4 (hbk)
0 946868 04 2 (pbk)

First published by W. & R. Chambers Ltd., Edinburgh, 1979

This edition published in Great Britain, 1988
by The Hardie Press
35 Mountcastle Terrace, Edinburgh, EH8 7SF

Music set by Philip Bowden Smith, Dalmally, Argyll
with emendations by Barry Peter Ould.

To the memory of
SANDY MILNE
of Banchory (1895-1979)

CONTENTS

INTRODUCTION

FOREWORD

I salute in my Scottish fiddler friends that innate urge to be audible,
visible and recognisable to our clan for what we are and what we feel.
Their music knows no detour—it goes straight to our feet if dance
we must, to our eyes if cry we must and always directly to our hearts
evoking every shade of joy, sorrow or contentment.

This music is living proof that the origins of all music are in our
pulse and in our voice and that the true and colourful folk heritage
and tradition must always remain at the very source of a culture and
of an organised, literate musical life, however erudite and complex
the structures may become.

The genuine Scottish fiddler has an infallible sense of rhythm,
never plays out of tune and is master of his distinctive and inimitable
style, which is more than can be said of most 'schooled' musicians.
We classical violinists have too obviously paid a heavy price for
being able to play with orchestras and follow a conductor.

May this thorough and well-documented collection of a people's
music serve to keep it alive in the song and dance and, above all, in
the hearts of those who will give our civilisation voice, spirit and
shape.

YEHUDI MENUHIN

PREFACE TO THE NEW EDITION

James Hunter's *The Fiddle Music of Scotland* first appeared in 1979. The torch so ably lit by Mr Hunter is now picked up and carried forth in this revised edition of the collection.

Our task has been three-fold: To produce fully-bowed versions of all the 365 melodies; to correct the errors and oversights a first edition is inevitably heir to; and finally to clarify that all-important ingredient in this music—the ornamentation.

This project could not have come to fruition without the help of several colleagues: Our grateful thanks go to Alastair Fyfe Holmes of W. & R. Chambers Ltd. for his professional help in facilitating the transfer of this title to the present publishers, and for his untiring personal assistance in relation to matters great and small. To Barry Peter Ould for his unflagging attention to detail while undertaking the emendations to the art-work, to Tom Anderson for permission to reproduce a copyright composition, and to Dr. David Johnson for providing invaluable advice on theoretical matters.

But above all we thank James Hunter who, whilst agreeing to this edition in the first place, has provided unfailing co-operation, courtesy and support throughout the whole process.

The Fiddle Music of Scotland is the most all-embracing collection of our national violin heritage undertaken this century. It is to be hoped that the new edition will continue to make this unique legacy available to an ever-widening and appreciative public.

ALASTAIR J. HARDIE, WILLIAM J. HARDIE,
Edinburgh
September, 1988.

INTRODUCTION

IN THE BEGINNING

Harp and fedyl both he fande
The getern and the sawtry
Lut and rybid ther gon gan,
Thair was al maner of mynstralsy.

THOMAS THE RHYMER

Stringed instruments, plucked or bowed, have existed in almost every country since the dawn of history. Of the many instruments mentioned in the poem the 'fedyl' or 'fethill' (fiddle) and the 'rybid' or 'rybybe' (rebec) were played by a bow. Together with another important early stringed instrument, the 'croud' or 'crwth', they were contributory ancestors of the violin. In Melrose Abbey, which was begun in 1136, there is a carving of a female figure bowing a rebec.

The early Stewart kings of Scotland were nearly all well disposed to music, having about their courts 'baith lute and harp and sindry other instrumentis of musick' ('trumpetis', 'fithelaris', 'clarscharis', and 'piparis'). James IV especially was a skilled performer on lute and clavichord, and both James V and Mary, Queen of Scots were enthusiastic amateurs. Pierre de Bourdeilles de Brantôme, a French historian and soldier who came to Scotland with Mary's Court, wrote that in August 1561 while he was staying at Holyrood 'there came under Her [Mary's] window, five or six hundred citizens of the town, who gave her a concert of the vilest fiddles and little rebecs, which are as bad as they can be in that country . . . so wretchedly out of tune and concord that nothing could be worse.' John Knox, the religious reformer, reporting the same event, alleges that 'the melody liked her well, and she willed the same to be continued'. Suffice it to say that Mary was reported to have changed her apartments immediately to a different part of the Palace!

The Royal Courts were, of course, at the heart of early artistic patronage. Monarchs maintained their own musicians during the seasons at the various Royal residences—Holyrood, Falkland and Linlithgow. Some of the musicians were French or English but the majority were Scots—fiddlers like Rankine, Boyd, Widderspune, and lutenists and violers such as Hume, Feldies, Dows and Hays.

The dances at court were confined mainly to Basse Dances, Pavans and Branles, updated from time to time with French importations, dances 'brent new frae France'. The viol, the main precursor of the violin, became the instrument of court and of 'polite society', and much splendid music was written 'apt for viols and voices'.

However, from literature of the fifteenth and sixteenth centuries there is evidence of the co-existence of a more popular oral

A woodcarving from south-west Scotland, showing a 'fitheler' of c. 1600.

National Museum of Antiquities of Scotland

tradition. For example, many references to song and dance tunes are made in the fifteenth-century poem 'Peblis to the Play' and the boisterous vernacular poem 'Cockelbie's Sow'. Both William Dunbar (1465–1530) and Sir David Lyndsay of the Mount (1490–1555) refer to the playing of 'springs'—quick, lively, dance tunes. The early lute manuscripts—the Rowallan (1615), the Skene (1620), the Straloch (1628) and the Guthrie (c.1660)—and the Blaikie manuscript for the viol family—all contain 'traditional' native airs alongside their courtly counterparts, further emphasising the dualism of Scottish music.

Around the time of the Restoration (1660) viols were supplanted by the violin as we know it today. As soon as it arrived, the Scots took to it—and it has gone on to become, with the bagpipe, one of our two national instruments.

One of the main reasons for the immediate impact of the violin in Scotland was that local craftsmen diligently copied the famous Italian models, particularly those of Amati and Guarnerius, thus founding a craft that still flourishes today. Violins were brought within the range of all social classes, for they were comparatively cheap. Even at the turn of this century they could be bought in some parts of Scotland for less than twenty pence. Sandy Milne, the well-known Banchory fiddler, recalled buying his first fiddle in 1903 for 'the price of five rabbits—and that included the green baize bag in which the traditional fiddler carried his instrument.'

In many ways the arrival of the violin in Scotland towards the end of the seventeenth century was fortuitously well-timed, for the eighteenth century saw a tremendous boom in native arts in Scotland, particularly dancing. The violin, with its incisive rhythmic attack, flexibility and potential tonal and dynamic contrasts was ideally suited for accompanying the new craze.

Gone were the Basse Dances, Branles and other courtly favourites. The Acts of 1649 and 1701 passed by the Church prohibiting 'promiscuous dancing' were swept aside and in place of the Court dances there arose the Scottish Reel, the Scottish Measure, the Country Dance and an English importation, the classically-based Minuet. In the 1760s came the unique crowning achievement of Scottish dancing—the Strathspey. All these dances were accompanied by traditional folk tunes. Fiddlers, dancing masters and numerous dilettantes soon swelled the existing repertoire to such good effect that eighteenth-century fiddle music has rightly become a cherished heirloom.

THE GOLDEN AGE

As is the common practice in other indigenous cultures, fiddle music was originally transmitted aurally. Very few records exist of compositions directly attributable to the earliest known fiddlers such as James Widderspune 'fithele that told tales and brocht fowles to the King' (James IV), the Cabroch 'fidlar', Muckart, the Browns of Kincardine and Strathspey and the Cummings of Freuchie.

One of the earliest tunes associated with itinerant or mendicant

fiddlers is *The Auld Man's Meer's Deid* by Patrick (Patie) Birnie (c.1635–1721) of Kinghorn on the Firth of Forth. Patie also wrote the words for this marvellously witty song. But undoubtedly the best example is *Macpherson's Rant*, composed by the notorious fiddler and freebooter James Macpherson on the eve of his execution at the market cross of Banff in 1700. This tune, as befits one aurally transmitted, abounds in a number of variants.

However, from about the turn of the eighteenth century it became customary practice for fiddlers to copy their own personal repertoire of tunes meticulously into small oblong manuscript books. Many of these still survive to the present day, and the writer possesses a few. The most famous of the early manuscripts is probably the Drummond Castle manuscript of 1734, transcribed by David Young for the Duke of Perth. It contains the earliest written records of such well-known tunes as *Tullochgorum* and *Caber Feidh*. To a certain extent this 'freezing' of folk music on to the printed page might well have eliminated the essential and attractive variants which arise from the vagaries of aural transmission. This fortunately did not happen. The Gows, in the introduction to the second part of their *Complete Repository of the Original Scotch Slow Strathspeys and Dances* (1802), remark that 'in every part of Scotland where we have occasionally been, and from every observation we were able to make, [we] have not once met with two professional musicians who played the same notes of any tune'.

The first printed collections to include a 'Scotch Dance' were published in England. John Playford included a number in *The English Dancing Master* (1651) and his son Henry published in 1700 a collection entirely devoted to Scottish tunes—*A Collection of Original Scotch Tunes (Full of Highland Humours)* for the violin. Scottish publishers soon followed suit, among them Adam Craig (1730), James Oswald (c.1740) and William McGibbon (1742–1768). Most collections were designed to be played by the violin or German flute with a bass for violoncello or harpsichord.

The first publication of fiddle music *per se* was a collection of 'Scots Reels or Country Dances' published in Edinburgh by Robert Bremner (1757). A profusion of collections followed from all over the country, most of them including original compositions in the traditional style. First to appear were those of Neil Stewart of Edinburgh (1761), John Riddell of Ayr (c.1766) and Daniel Dow of Edinburgh (whose collection of 1776 was the first to include the word 'strathspey' in its title). These were followed by the collections of Joshua Campbell of Glasgow (1779), Alexander 'King' McGlashan of Edinburgh (1780), Angus Grant of Grantown (1780), Isaac Cooper of Banff (1783), John Bowie of Perth (1785), Robert Riddell of Glenriddell (1787), Malcolm McDonald of Inver (1788), Robert Petrie of Kirkmichael (1790), Archibald Duff of Montrose (1794) and John Morison of Peterhead (1797).

Abune them a', however, are the collections of the great masters of the period—Niel Gow and his son Nathaniel, Robert Mackintosh, William Marshall—and Captain Simon Fraser's great work, *The Airs and Melodies Peculiar to the Highlands of Scotland*, published in 1815.

Patie Birnie, 1635-1721. An engraving after a contemporary portrait.
Scottish National Portrait Gallery

One interesting feature of this, the most prolific period of fiddle-music writing, was the patronage afforded to the fiddler by the aristocracy and landed gentry. They subscribed to the collections (many, in fact, were the dedicatees) and some contained compositions from the pen of these aristrocratic amateurs such as Colonel Hugh Montgomerie, twelfth Earl of Eglintoun, Sir Alexander Don of Newton Don, Sir Alexander Boswell of Auchinleck and Miss Lucy Johnston of Hilton.

MAJOR COMPOSERS

A detail from David Allan's 'The Highland Dance'. Niel Gow is the fiddler in this painting, with his brother Donald playing the cello.
National Galleries of Scotland

Niel Gow was born at Inver, a hamlet near Dunkeld, on 22 March 1727. Son of a plaid weaver, Niel (he always spelt his name with the *i* before the *e* in Gaelic fashion) started the violin at the age of nine and was virtually self-taught, apart from some instruction when he was thirteen from John Cameron, a servant of the Stewarts of Grantully. In 1745, as Bonnie Prince Charlie was raising his standard at Glenfinnan to begin his ill-fated campaign, Niel won a competition in Perth open to all Scotland. He won, a contemporary report said, 'with the cheerful consent of the other competitors'. The judge, a blind man named John McCraw, declared that 'he could distinguish Niel's bow amang a hunder players'. A powerful upstroke and his ability 'to lift the bow smartly off the string with a peculiar jerk of the wrist' made Niel famous throughout Scotland. He was a man of 'open, honest and pleasing countenance, and a homely, easy and unaffected manner, accompanied by a perfect honesty and integrity of thought and action, placing him on a footing of familiarity and independence in the presence of the proudest of the land'. Niel was patronised by three Dukes of Atholl during his long life. A professional musician—'the best fiddler that ever kittled thairm with horse hair'—he was much in demand to play at important balls and parties, and could command a considerable fee. Records show that the fee for a normal fiddler of the time was about two shillings and sixpence to five shillings (plus a shilling for 'ale money'). Niel's fee was fifteen shillings, sometimes higher, depending on the importance of the occasion. Stories and anecdotes, mainly apocryphal, abounded about him. He was, and is, a legend.

Gow the composer wrote about eighty-seven tunes. It is difficult to be certain of the exact number, because Niel was guilty on occasion of blatant plagiarism. However, besides strathspeys and reels, jigs, etc., he wrote some of the best elegiac pieces in the repertoire, for example his *Lamentation for James Moray of Abercarney* and *Lament for the Death of his Second Wife*.

He died on 1 March 1807 at Inver, his home during most of his eighty years.

Nathaniel Gow, the fourth son of Niel Gow, was born at Inver on 28 May 1763. Like his elder brothers William, John and Andrew, he was taught by his father on the kit (a kind of small fiddle) then sent to Edinburgh to study with Robert Mackintosh and Alexander

'King' McGlashan, so-called because of his majestic, stately appearance and showy dress. Nathaniel inherited his father's talents as a violinist, but with his superior education he was the better all-round musician of the two. He studied the cello under Joseph Reinagle, who became Professor of Music at Oxford. He also played the trumpet, and in 1782 was appointed one of His Majesty's Herald Trumpeters of Scotland.

In 1791 he succeeded his brother William as the leader of the orchestra that played at the fashionable concerts in Edinburgh, especially the Caledonian Hunt Balls and Assemblies. Nathaniel was the leading musical figure in the capital and, like his father, was absent from few really fashionable functions. The aristocracy showered him with gifts, and George IV granted him a pension. He was at one time reputed to be worth twenty thousand pounds. In 1796, in partnership with William Shepherd, he started an extensive music-publishing business. Nathaniel claimed to have written a hundred and ninety-seven tunes but, regrettably, he was even more guilty of plagiarism than his father, especially of Marshall's music. He was, however, a fine composer of original melodies, and his authenticated compositions show culture, variety and sophistication. His strathspey *Lady Charlotte Campbell* and the reels *Loch Earn* and *Largo's Fairy Dance* are in the standard repertoire of any respected fiddler.

Robert Mackintosh, born in Tullymet about 1745, is the least documented of the great Scottish fiddle composers. He was an excellent performer and he was considered by contemporaries to be Niel Gow's most serious rival. In 1773 he settled in Edinburgh, advertising himself as a musician. His charge for lessons was one guinea per quarter 'for the public class', and one guinea per month 'for a private hour'. For three years 'Red Rob', as he was known because of his fiery red hair, resided in Aberdeen and led the band there at the Gentlemen's Concerts. He then returned to Edinburgh and in 1803 moved to London, where he died in 1807.

He published four volumes of his music, and the best of his tunes, *Miss Campbell of Saddell* and the strathspey and reel *Lady Charlotte Campbell*, show to the full his elegant style—and his fondness for flat keys.

William Marshall, the most prodigiously talented fiddle composer of the eighteenth century, was born at Fochabers on 27 December 1748, the third of a large family. The only formal education he received was six months at the parish school and a few lessons from one of the staff at Gordon Castle, where he started at the age of twelve as assistant to the house steward. In due course he rose to become butler to the fourth Duke of Gordon, and then estates factor to his successor, the 'Cock o' the North', the fifth and last Duke.

Marshall was a sort of Admirable Crichton. In addition to composing music, he studied mechanics, astronomy, architecture, land surveying and clockmaking, and was a respected athlete and dancer. He was a highly esteemed player of Scottish Music, his style

William Marshall, 1748-1833, 'the first composer of strathspeys of the age'.

Scottish National Portrait Gallery

'A Dancing Lesson at Hopetoun House', an engraving after Frederick Tayler. The Scottish nobility continued to patronise traditional music—and to employ fiddlers as dancing masters—until well into the nineteenth century. *Scottish National Portrait Gallery*

being characterised by 'fullness of intonation, precision, and brilliance of expression'. Certainly as a composer he fully merited Burns's accolade as 'the first composer of strathspeys of the age'. He was in a sense an intuitive composer. His compositions came suddenly to him 'as a result of momentary whim or fitful inspiration. They cost him no labour, and once he had hit upon a rhythm he seldom retouched it.' Many of his airs have a wide compass; many are in flat keys. When questioned about their difficulty he replied that 'he did not write music for bunglers'. In general he made less use of gapped scales and double tonics than the Gows, and his music is more rooted in the ordinary major/minor modes.

His strathspeys in particular are more regular in their formal construction; they have a buoyancy and easy natural flow about them. Such strathspeys as *The Marchioness of Huntly*, *The Marquis of Huntly's Farewell*, and *Craigellachie Brig* (where the double tonic is used to magnificent effect) testify to his mastery of this form.

He wrote two hundred and fifty-seven tunes, and published two volumes in 1781 and 1822, the latter a collection unequalled in sustained quality before or since.

Marshall died, universally esteemed, on 29 May 1833 at Dandaleith, and his death closed one of the great periods of Scottish traditional music.

THE NINETEENTH CENTURY

Fashion, especially in music, has always had peaks and troughs. By 1820 the great fiddle era was past. High society, which had so ardently patronised and supported traditional music and dancing, turned to new fashions and new dances. Quadrilles, polkas, waltzes and even mazurkas were the new order of the day. Only dances like the Foursome Reel, the Reel of Tulloch, and the Eightsome Reel held their place firmly at society balls. Fiddle music retreated, for the moment, to the grass roots of indigenous culture—at country weddings, kirns, fireside ceilidhs, hiring fairs and the like. But some of the landed gentry kept faith with the fiddler and a certain amount of patronage still existed, especially in Perthshire. Many fine players carried on the tradition, among them Airchie Allan of Forfar (1794–1837) and his cousin James Allan (1800–1877), who always billed himself 'Reel Player to the Earl of Airlie'; the 'Fiddling Tinker' Pate Baillie (1774–1841) of Liberton; Charles Grant (1810–1892) of Aberlour; the MacIntoshes of Dunkeld; the Atholl fiddler Duncan McKerracher (1796–1873)—the so-called 'Dunkeld Paganini'—and the 'Tarland Minstrel' Peter Milne (1824–1908). But the focal point of traditional fiddle music was to shift from Perthshire to the north-east of Scotland. It was there that it reached its peak of popularity in the late nineteenth century, mainly through the career of one man who was to make it commercially successful—the self-styled 'Strathspey King', James Scott Skinner.

Scott Skinner was born on 5 August 1843 in Banchory, into a fiddling family. His father, after losing three fingers of his left hand in a shooting accident, learned to play left-handed, and became a

prominent dancing master on Deeside.

His son James was born, it was said, 'with a pen in his ear and a fiddle stick in his hand'. He was first taught to play fiddle and cello by, in his own words, 'the most rigorous of taskmasters', his elder brother Sandy. But despite an alleged 'lack o' glegness in the uptak'' he was soon trotting out with his brother and the 'Tarland Minstrel' Peter Milne to play at barns and bothy dances in the neighbourhood. At the age of ten he set off to Manchester to join 'Dr. Mark's Little Men'—the most famous juvenile orchestra of the day. There he had lessons with the French violinist Charles Rougier who was a member of the Hallé Orchestra. At nineteen, Skinner won a big fiddle competition in Inverness, competing against the great fiddlers of the day, and played so brilliantly that the Chief Judge, Cluny Macpherson, uttered the now famous prophetic words, 'Gentlemen, we have never before heard the like of this from a beardless boy. This boy will be heard of some day.' This was the first of many competitions Skinner won. The writer recalls an amusing story told to him by Hector MacAndrew about an old Banchory worthy who met Scott Skinner's brother Sandy the day after an important competition in Edinburgh. Sandy was also a fine exponent and when asked how he had got on he replied, 'Very well, I am home with the gold medal in my pocket—and my brother James was there too!'

Scott Skinner made a comfortable living as a teacher and dancing master around the north of Scotland, and one patronage he especially prized was that of teaching the children of Queen Victoria's tenantry at Balmoral. He toured extensively, even to America, and his concerts were enthusiastically acclaimed. Like some fiddlers a century and a half before him, he often played a mixed programme of classical and traditional music. Here is an extract from a concert review from the old Inverness paper *The Highlander* of 4 April 1879: 'Mr. Skinner really does the instrument justice. His performance of Mozart's *Figaro*, Paganini's *Rondo Pizzicato*, and De Beriot's concerto were simply magnificent. And when he turned to the Strathspeys and Reels, oh, what spirit and what finish.' Skinner is the only one of the legendary fiddlers of the past to record his music for posterity, and some of these recordings have recently been re-issued.

He was the most prolific of all the fiddler composers with over six hundred pieces in print, including virtuosic showpieces. Many of his compositions show his better training as a violinist—with the use of the high positions, left hand pizzicato, frequent double stopping, and a chromaticism that bounds free of the old Scottish modes.

He died on 17 March 1927, the last of the really great fiddle composers.

John Robertson of Broxburn: a Scottish fiddle-maker at work in the 1890s.
Country Life Archive, National Museum of Antiquities of Scotland

THE TWENTIETH CENTURY

The beginning of this century saw a continuing decline in interest in fiddle music, certainly in the numbers of those participating. The

upheavals of the first half of the century made it difficult for fiddle music to flourish. The effect of two wars resulted in a radical change in society's interests and habits. New dances, mainly of American origin, became the new rage. Mechanisation, the advent of radio, television and the record industry, considerably lessened the need or desire for 'homespun entertainment'. Fiddle music continued to survive, of course, in various pockets throughout the country. James Henry of Macduff, James F. Dickie of New Deer, George Wright of Turriff, Joseph Johnston of Rattray, the Hardie family of Methlick and the Camerons of Kirriemuir were all fine exponents—and there was that kenspeckle figure 'Dancie' Reid, a dancing master and bandleader in the Kirriemuir area. Alex Young, an old fiddler living at Glamis and a pupil of Dancie's, tells of the day his teacher was dismissed by a local farmer for spending too much of his employer's time playing the fiddle. 'Dancie' made his farewell playing and dancing the Highland Fling all the way down the turnip field, flicking the turnips out of the drills with his feet as he went, finishing with a final flourish—on top of the dung-heap!

Country-dancing has to a large extent been revitalised through the efforts of the Royal Scottish Country Dance Society, which was founded in 1923. Unfortunately the violin has been ousted by the accordion as the main accompanying instrument for the dance. But the tradition lives on through such fine players as Bill Hardie, Angus Cameron, Arthur Robertson, Ron Gonella and Hector MacAndrew—the finest living exponent, who can trace his fiddling lineage directly back to Niel Gow. His grandfather was taught by Niel's last pupil, James MacIntosh of Dunkeld.

Although the future of fiddle music may have looked bleak at the turn of the century, the outlook today is much brighter. In the past decade, coinciding with a re-awakening of Scottish nationhood, there has been a dramatic resurgence of interest. In 1969 the BBC ran a competition which attracted over a hundred and fifty entries. Since then numerous other competitions have been established, and many are being won by very promising players of the younger generation. Old Strathspey and Reel Societies have been re-invigorated, and new ones have been formed. A recent phenomenon first seen in Oban—the Fiddle Rally, in which members of various societies join forces to form orchestras numbering up to three hundred—has attracted large and enthusiastic audiences. The media are taking note, record sales are booming. Fiddle music is in the limelight again.

FIDDLE MUSIC IN SHETLAND

The indigenous music of Shetland is, strictly speaking, culturally different from the music of mainland Scotland. Its origins lie more in Scandinavia. Indeed Shetland (the name derives from Norse *Hjaltland*) was part of Norway until annexed to Scotland in 1612.

Before the arrival of the violin the stringed instrument used in Shetland was the *gué*—the Shetland equivalent of the *crwth*. One of

its main technical characteristics was the use of unstopped strings as drones producing a sound not dissimilar to the sympathetic strings of its Norse counterpart, the *Hardangerfele* (Hardanger fiddle). The tradition of ringing strings above and below the melody line is a characteristic of Shetland fiddle playing which is still practised today, especially by the older players. One particularly distinctive feature of these older players is that they did not hold the fiddle as it is held today: they held it well down on the chest. What was even more remarkable was that they did not draw the bow straight across from G string to E string. Instead the bow stayed more or less on an even course and it was the fiddle which moved. Such a technique resulted in a rich harmonic texture as the open strings were kept ringing both above and below the melody line. The driven bow, so fundamental to the technique of the mainland player, was never used in Shetland.

The tunes, and their titles, reflect the rich cultural life of the islands, where music played a natural part at various celebrations—such as New Year, Christmas, weddings and regattas. The Muckle Reel and Auld Reel have a strong affinity with the Norwegian *Halling*, while the quick reels show an Irish influence. Such influences are not surprising when one remembers that Shetland has been a centre for northern whaling and fishing fleets for centuries. It was not uncommon for Shetlanders to take their fiddles to sea with them to while away the time on these often long and arduous voyages. No doubt they met and exchanged tunes with fellow fo'c'sle fiddlers from other sailing nations. (Greenland skippers, for example, always carried fiddlers on board to entertain the crews.) Also, during the annual herring season, workers from the south went to the islands to work in the shore-based industries such as gutting, packing and salting down the herring—and they brought their own cultural influence. Early this century the phonograph and gramophone records of the mainland virtuosos Scott Skinner and McKenzie Murdoch introduced new techniques and styles.

No matter what the origins and influences, Shetland has absorbed them all in music which is unique and altogether different from the mainland style. It is a tradition which the Shetlanders guard tenaciously and proudly. They have a strong Folk Society (founded 1945) which, besides having its own traditional fiddle band, has rescued and documented much valuable material. (The School of Scottish Studies at the University of Edinburgh has also contributed greatly to recording Shetland culture.) The Zetland Education Committee has shown an enlightened awareness of the island's heritage by appointing instructors solely to teach indigenous fiddle music.

Like the mainland, Shetland has a long and distinguished fiddling history, with noted players of bygone days such as Laurence Laurenson ('Singing Lowrie'), John Gaudie, Willie Bairnson and John Moffat. Today Tom Anderson, M.B.E., Willie Hunter, Aly Bain and many others are executants of the highest quality. But it is not only playing that continues to flourish: composers are very active, writing tunes equal to anything being composed at present both in quantity and quality.

The music-makers of an Angus bothy, c. 1910.
Country Life Archive, National Museum of Antiquities of Scotland

THE SCOTTISH IDIOM

There are undoubtedly melodic clichés and various rhythmical 'fingerprints' which make Scottish music immediately recognisable as such. But at a deeper level it is the use of the old 'gapped scales' and ecclesiastical modes which gives it its inherent and distinctive flavour.

GAPPED SCALES

There are two species of gapped scale:

1 The pentatonic, or five-note, scale

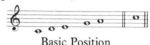

Basic Position

This scale has two gaps and the smallest interval is a tone. It is not only in Scotland that this scale was used as a basis for folk music: it was also used by civilisations as far apart as China, Africa and Lapland. The scale is thought by musicologists to be vocal rather than instrumental in origin. Well-known songs such as *Auld Lang Syne* and *Roy's Wife of Aldivalloch* are pentatonic in construction.

2 The hexatonic, or six-note, scale

Basic Position   Basic Position

This scale is derived by filling in *one* of the gaps of the pentatonic scale. It therefore exists in two forms, the important difference being the position of the semitone. Many tunes are rooted in this scale, e.g. *Whistle O'er The Lave O't*, *Ca' the Yowes*, *Gala Water*, etc.

THE ECCLESIASTICAL OR CHURCH MODES

Ionian   Dorian

Phrygian   Lydian

Mixo-Lydian   Aeolian

The modes are set out here with reference to the same tonic; the semitones are marked by slurs.

An understanding of these modes, and the gapped scales and their inversions, is crucial to the comprehending of the folk-music idiom, since they form the constructional basis of so much of European folk music. The important thing to realise is that our major and minor scales are identical in construction whatever the key, varying only in pitch. The modes/gapped scales and their inversions are not keys: the arrangement of tones and semitones is

An old itinerant fiddler, from a nineteenth-century engraving.
Scottish National Portrait Gallery

different in each one, and it is precisely this difference that gives each mode its distinct feel or flavour. Imbuing them with classical harmony robs them of their beauty.

Another strong influence in the construction of Scottish folk melodies is the bagpipe scale, and the triads to be found within it.

Melodies based on oscillating triads either a tone above or below the tonic triad are common. *Miss Stewart of Grantully*, *Tullochgorum*, *Link Him Dodie*, *The Inverness Gathering*, *Angus Campbell* and *The Laird o' Drumblair* are all good examples. The flattened-seventh triad alternating with the tonic was a particular favourite. This formula is sometimes referred to as a 'double tonic'.

MISS ANNY STEWART, BOHALLY

Glenesk fiddler, 1880s.
Country Life Archive, National Museum of Antiquities of Scotland

HINTS ON BOWING TECHNIQUE

Dr. McKnight, writing in the *Scots Magazine* of 1809 on the second anniversary of Niel Gow's death, suggested that there was perhaps no species of music which depended so much on bowing to give it its true character than the Highland Strathspey and Reel. Another of Gow's contemporaries, Alexander Campbell, wrote in 1802 that '[Gow's] manner of playing his native airs is faithful, correct, and spirited. He slurs none, but plays distinctly, with accuracy, precision, and *peculiar accentuation*.'

The peculiar accentuation referred to is probably the jerk of the wrist on the upstroke of the bow which gives the distinctive accent to the strathspey rhythm. It is the use of such techniques that distinguishes the traditional fiddler from the more formal, classically-trained violinist.

These tricks of technique are found mostly in the playing of the strathspey, the most characteristic form of Scottish traditional music. It is a slow dance, closely allied to the faster reel, and derives its name from the strath or valley of the River Spey, where it was first danced. Its music is in four-in-a-measure time with a definite dotted rhythm.

The most frequent rhythm is the dotted quaver followed by the semiquaver,

and there are four main methods of treating it.

1 HACK-BOWING

Hack-bowing is the term used to describe the use of a down-bow on the dotted quaver followed by the up-bow on the semiquaver. It is

effective only when used sparingly—its continual use tends to give the music a monotonous, jerky effect.

2 SNAP-BOWING

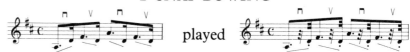

Snap-bowing is one of the most fundamental strokes in strathspey playing and mastery of it is essential if the player is to capture the rhythmic drive inherent in the music. It is indicated nowadays by the use of the 'straight slur', although Peter Milne, the 'Tarland Minstrel', often used his own sign when indicating snap-bowing:

In each case the bow should be moved in the same direction for both notes, either up or down, with the shortest stoppage of the bow between the dotted quaver and the semiquaver. This means that the semiquaver is cleanly detached.

The ordinary slur is employed when a more *legato* effect is desired but it is used to its best effect in cross-bowing.

3 CROSS-BOWING

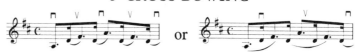

In contrast to the previous examples, cross-bowing gives a *legato* rather than a *staccato* effect to the long–short rhythm. When used sparingly it adds variety and interest to the phrasing, especially in melodies which tend to be repetitive in structure.

4 BACK-BOWING

Back-bowing is the term used for the employment of an up-bow, generally in the strong beat of the bar. It is very effective for two purposes: (a) to secure good accent; (b) to correct the direction of the bow.

THE SCOTS SNAP
When the long–short rhythm is reversed—

—it is known as the *Scots Snap*. The Scots Snap is undoubtedly the most instantly recognisable of the Scottish melodic/rhythmic fingerprints. It has been unjustly maligned mainly because of its over-use in *English* music halls when, combined with the flattened seventh, it provided 'instant Scotch'! It is a crucial element in the rhythmic structure of the strathspey, and an essential part of the folk musician's armoury. The Scots Snap consists of a semiquaver (on the beat) followed by a dotted quaver (occupying the rest of the beat). It is played with separate bow-strokes, the dotted quaver being taken *staccato* and the bow lifted smartly off the strings, thus giving the 'snap' effect. The ability to 'lift the bow smartly off the strings with a peculiar jerk of the wrist' was one of the main features of Niel Gow's playing.

THE UP-DRIVEN BOW

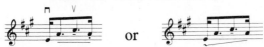

A further development of the Scots Snap is the up-driven bow (sometimes simply called the driven bow) in which the first stroke is taken smartly down, leaving the up-bow to take the remaining three notes. Thus the complete movement consists of one down-bow followed by three up-bows. Extra bow pressure is put on the third note of the phrase to re-emphasise the rhythm—hence the 'driven' nature of the stroke—and the last note, the semiquaver, is taken *staccato*. It was the favourite stroke of Niel Gow, whose up-bow was reputed to be uncommonly powerful. 'Where a note produced by the up-bow was often feeble and indistinct in other hands, it was struck in [Gow's] playing with a strength and certainty which never failed to surprise and delight the hearer.' When played well, the driven bow certainly gives the whole strathspey a bolder and more distinctive character.

A detail from 'The Penny Wedding' by David Allan. Country-dancers at a rural wedding of the late eighteenth century.
National Galleries of Scotland

Here are two typical examples from well known strathspeys:

THE BRAES O' MAR

THE BRIDGE OF DEE

THE DOWN-DRIVEN BOW

The down-driven bow is a very effective stroke but opportunities for its use are much more limited than those for the up-driven bow. It generally occurs at the ends of a strong phrase, and extra bow pressure is applied to the note following the crotchet—in the example above, the semiquaver.

THE SWINGING OR LONG BOW

The swinging bow, or long bow, can be taken as an up or down

bow-stroke and it actually does give a swinging effect to the phrasing. In the four-note groups above, the last semiquaver is *staccato*. This stroke is best used to give a longer and more varied phrase pattern to repetitive melodic phrases.

UNISONS

Unisons are played to give additional power and force to the bolder tunes. They are effected by sounding simultaneously the note on the open string with the note of the same pitch on the string below. Since the first position is the normal position for playing the older airs, unison playing involves the frequent use of the fourth finger, or 'crannie' as it is often called in the North-East. A typical example of the use of unisons is a passage such as this·

Double stopping and the use of ringing open strings are not as prevalent on the mainland as in Shetland. They are, however, frequently used to add fire and character to the more forceful phrases. For example a phrase such as

may be played

or

can be played

SYNCOPATED TRIPLET

The use of a syncopated triplet

in lieu of an ordinary triplet

is a subtlety developed mainly in the North-East. Particularly fine exponents of it were George Wright of Turriff and James F. Dickie of New Deer.

Whilst it does add great rhythmic vitality to the phrase, it should be sparingly used and crisply executed.

'A Dance in a Barn'.
A watercolour sketch by David Allan (1744-1796) depicting 'homespun entertainment' in the golden age of the fiddle.
National Galleries of Scotland

STRAIGHT AND LOOPED TIES

These two signs, the invention of Scott Skinner, are mainly used at the end of phrases. The straight tie (on the left) indicates that the second note is to be re-emphasised with the bow travelling in the same direction.

The loop (on the right) again has the second note re-emphasised, often resulting in an accented ending to a phrase or tune.

THE DOODLE

The 'doodle' was the nickname of a melodic cliché often found in the older strathspeys. It consisted of the grouping together of four successive notes of the same pitch. This century it has fallen out of favour, modern players substituting the 'Scots Snap'.

Highland Whisky as written

as played today

SCORDATURA

The device of *scordatura*—the altering of the tuning of the strings to facilitate the execution of difficult intervals, was often used by the older fiddlers. Directions for re-tuning were generally given at the beginning of the music,

e.g.

although itinerant fiddlers, who had little recourse to the printed page, were already acquainted with the device which they had picked up orally from their predecessors. The tuning of the bottom two strings of the violin up a tone to A and E respectively was the most common re-tuning, and strathspeys such as *Dunkeld House* and *Hamilton House* were played in this way. A good example is the third measure of the old reel *Greig's Pipes*, which sounds thus:

But with the violin re-tuned to A/E/A/E, the fiddler actually plays it as:

When played, the open G string sounds A and the D string sounds E. Of course, the melody *sounds* exactly the same as the previous example, but it is much easier to execute! *Scordatura* tuning eliminates the need for cross-fingering with the first finger (to play

Fife farmworker with fiddle, 1900. Self-taught fiddlers like this man provided the music for local 'maidens', or harvest festivals.
Country Life Archive, National Museum of Antiquities of Scotland

successive A and E) and the open strings give the melody a resonant ring.

Grace-notes and *ornamentation* are part and parcel of Scottish music. Each fiddler tends to have his own particular form of embellishment, and it is this, together with his bowing technique, that gives his music its own individuality. Since ornamentation is a matter of personal taste it is difficult to lay down any definite rules, beyond the fact that when ornaments are played they should be fluently and neatly insinuated. When well done, they bring the music alive.

There are many other subtle tricks of technique employed by the traditional fiddler, most of which are difficult, if not impossible, to communicate on the printed page. Where and when to use them—and the various bowing techniques—in order to obtain the maximum musical effect, can only be learnt from direct contact with a good exponent. For while there are many things one can pick up just by listening, there are certain things—particularly in bowing—which can be assimilated only through the eye. As Scott Skinner so succinctly put it: 'The tune on the printed page is simply a skeleton. You must catch the character by contagion!'

An Aberdeenshire 'bothy band' of 1915, from an early postcard.
Country Life Archive, National Museum of Antiquities of Scotland

ALPHABETICAL LIST OF TUNES

xxv

The autograph manuscript of a pastoral by Scott Skinner
complete with the composer's own annotations. *Peterhead Arbuthnot Museum*

AIRS AND PASTORALS

1
MISS GRAHAM OF INCHBRAKIE

Grandly ♪ = 76

Nath. Gow

2
MISS LUCY JOHNSTON'S COMPLIMENTS
TO NIEL GOW

Gracefully ♪ = 80

L. Johnston

MAIRI BHAN OG: MARY, YOUNG AND FAIR

3

MRS. HAMILTON OF PENCAITLAND

4

Nath. Gow

COILSFIELD HOUSE

5

Nath. Gow

LADY ANN HOPE'S FAVOURITE

Niel Gow

Tenderly ♪ =80

LAMENT FOR THE DEATH
OF THE REV. ARCHIE BEATON

J. Mason

Slow and Pathetic ♩ = 58

Auld Robin Gray

Rev. W. Leeves

I gang like a ghaist and I carena to spin,
I darena think o' Jamie, for that wad be a sin;
But I'll do my best a gude wife to be,
For auld Robin Gray is kind to me.

Lady Anne Barnard

Slow, with Expression ♪ = 69

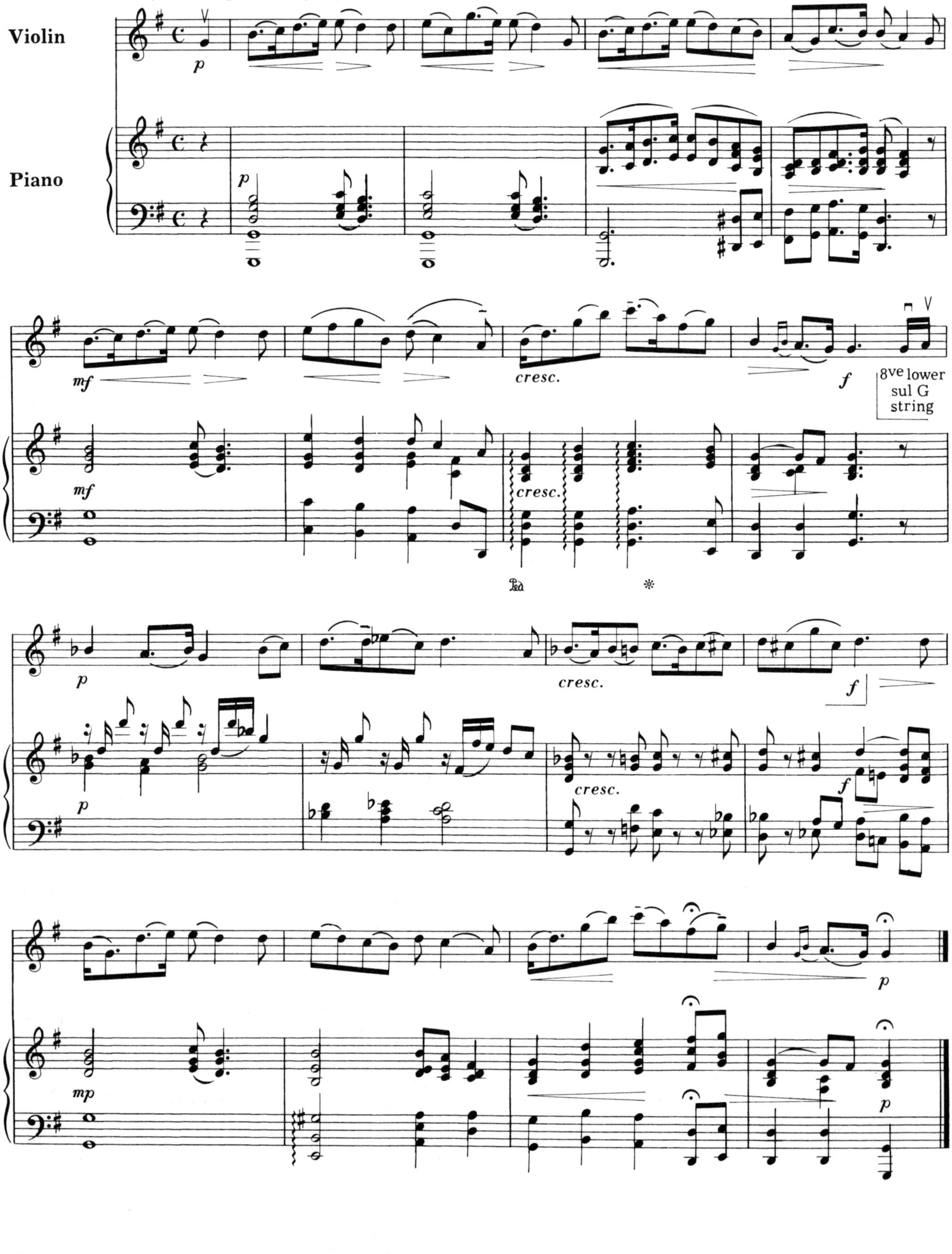

NIEL GOW'S LAMENTATION
FOR JAMES MORAY, ESQ., OF ABERCARNEY

Slow and Pathetic ♪ = 63

Niel Gow

mp

rall.

MACPHERSON'S RANT

J. Macpherson

Farewell, ye dungeons dark and strong,
The wretch's destinie!
MacPherson's time will not be long
On yonder gallows-tree.

*Sae rantingly, sae wantonly,
Sae dauntingly gaed he,
He play'd a spring, and danc'd it round
Below the gallows-tree.*

With Vigour ♩ = 120

BURNS

f

boldly

[Fine]

Da Capo

THE NAMELESS LASSIE

Wm. Marshall

Tenderly ♩ = 63

MRS. HELEN N. ROBERTSON

A. S. Robertson

With Expression ♩ = 72

SITTING IN THE STERN OF A BOAT

Rev. Wm. McLeod

With Longing ♪ = 69

THE BONNIE BANKS OF AYR

With Great Expression ♪ = 76

CAOIDH NA H'ALBA' AIRSON NIAL GOBHA: CALEDONIA'S WAIL FOR NIEL GOW—HER FAVOURITE MINSTREL

Capt. S. Fraser

Nae fabled wizard's wand, I trow,
Had e'er the magic airt o' Gow,
When wi' a wave he draws his bow
Across his wondrous fiddle!

BURNS

Stately ♩ = 46

16 CLUNY CASTLE (INVERNESS-SHIRE)

A. Troup

With Quiet Dignity ♪ = 69

17 THE HILLS OF LORNE

C. Hunter

Slow, with Feeling ♩ = 60

18 MAJOR GRAHAM OF INCHBRAKIE

Niel Gow

Elegantly ♩ = 52

Niel Gow's Lament
for the Death of his Second Wife

With Deep Feeling ♪ = 84

Niel Gow

Mrs. Scott Skinner

With Dignity ♩ = 46

J. S. Skinner

THE BONNIE LASS O' BON-ACCORD

Bold and Heroic ♩ = 58

J. S. Skinner: arr. J. M. Hunter

VAR. 1

VAR. 2 Minor—Sadly

22

BONNIE GLENFARG

J. S. Skinner

Sweetly ♪ = 100

THE BRAES OF AUCHTERTYRE

Slow and Stately ♩ = 44

Crockat: arr. J. S. Skinner

DARGAI

Pibroch—Adagio ♪ = 80

J. S. Skinner

THE FLOWER OF THE QUERN

Slow and Sustained ♩ = 48

J. S. Skinner: arr. J. M. Hunter

HECTOR [MacDonald] THE HERO

J. S. Skinner

O wail for the mighty in battle,
Loud lift ye the coronach strain,
For Hector, the hero, of deathless fame,
Will never come back again.

With Intense Sadness ♪ = 80

THE FALLEN CHIEF

Lament ♩ = 52

J. S. Skinner

LAMENT OF FLORA MACDONALD

With Expression and Flow ♪ = 92

Niel Gow Jnr.

MacGillamun's Oran Mor

Stately Larghetto ♪ = 88

G. MacIlwham

Mrs. Jamieson's Favourite

Gently ♪ = 88

C. Grant

MARGARET ANN ROBERTSON

Slow, with Expression ♩ = 76

F. R. Jamieson

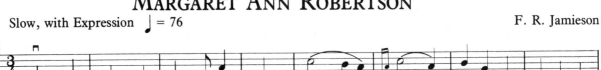

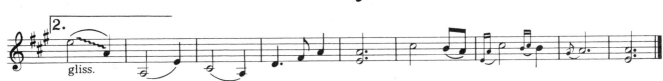

MRS. MAJOR L. STEWART OF THE ISLAND OF JAVA

With Dignity ♩ = 76

Wm. Marshall

DUNCAN DAVIDSON

40 MISS LAURA ANDREW

Elegantly ♩ = 69

J. S. Skinner

41 ANGUS CAMERON'S COMPLIMENTS TO ALEX WEBSTER

Slow, with Expression ♪ = 96

A. Cameron

42 MR. GARDEN OF TROUP'S FAREWELL TO FRANCE

Elegantly ♪ = 63

R. Petrie

THE AULD WIFE AYONT THE FIRE

Arr. J. M. Hunter

THE MARQUIS OF HUNTLY'S SNUFF MILL

With Measured Grace ♩ = 52

Wm. Marshall

GUN BHRIS MO CHRIDH O'N DH'FHALBH THU:
MY HEART IS BROKEN SINCE THY DEPARTURE

Slow and Pathetic ♪ = 80

46 THE DUCHESS OF MANCHESTER'S FAREWELL
TO THE HIGHLANDS OF SCOTLAND

Pastoral—March ♩ = 63

Wm. Marshall

neatly

47 FAREWELL TO WHISKY

Slow and Pathetic ♩ = 44

Niel Gow

48 GREIG'S

Majestic ♩ = 42

CHAPEL KEITHACK

Cantabile ♩ = 46

Wm. Marshall: arr. J. M. Hunter

50

THE DUCHESS OF BEDFORD

Wm. Marshall

Stately ♩ = 46

51

A Bhean An Tigh Nach Leig U Steach: Gudewife, Admit The Wanderer

With Hesitation and Impatience ♪ = 76

52

Huntly Lodge

Wm. Marshall

With Quiet Dignity ♩ = 50

53   NACH TRUAGH MO CHAS: HARD IS MY FATE

Slow and Plaintive ♩ = 58

54   LAMENT FOR SIR HARRY LUMSDEN, BART., OF AUCHINDOIR

Slow and Pathetic ♪ = 104

Wm. Marshall

55   PRINCE CHARLIE'S LAST VIEW OF SCOTLAND

Slow and Tender ♪ = 88

MISS WHARTON DUFF

56

Brightly ♩ = 80

Wm. Marshall: arr. J. M. Hunter

Violin

Piano

MISS CAMPBELL OF SADDELL

57

Gentle Pastoral ♩ = 58

Robt. Mackintosh

LADY MARY PRIMROSE

Nobly ♩ = 50

BARAIN CHULRABHAIG:
THE ANCIENT BARONS OF KILRAVOCK

Slow and Stately ♩ = 46

60

THE AULD BRIG O' DON

J. Henry

Slow, with Expression ♩ = 44

61

HO CHA NEIL MULAD OIRNN:
THE EMIGRANT'S FAREWELL

Slow and Tender ♩ = 44

62

ROSLIN CASTLE

Nobly, with Expression ♩ = 50

rall.   a tempo

THE MARCHIONESS OF HUNTLY'S FAVOURITE

Slow and Pathetic ♩ = 48

Wm. Marshall

THE WEEPING BIRCHES OF KILMORACK

Slow, with Intense Feeling ♩ = 72

J. S. Skinner

THE VALLEY OF SILENCE

Elegy—Adagio ♩ = 54

J. S. Skinner

SLAN GUN D'THIG MO RUN A NALL: WELL MAY MY TRUE LOVE ARRIVE

Slow, with Expression ♪ = 80

MISS LYALL

As played by Angus Cameron

67

MISS [SARAH] DRUMMOND OF PERTH

68

Taobh Tuath nan Garbh Bheann:
North of the Grampians

Capt. S. Fraser

Captain Campbell

The Brig o' Potarch

J. S. Skinner

THE CLAYMORE

A. Cameron

THE DUKE OF GORDON'S BIRTHDAY

Wm. Marshall:
as played by Douglas Lawrence

THE HAUGHS o' CROMDALE

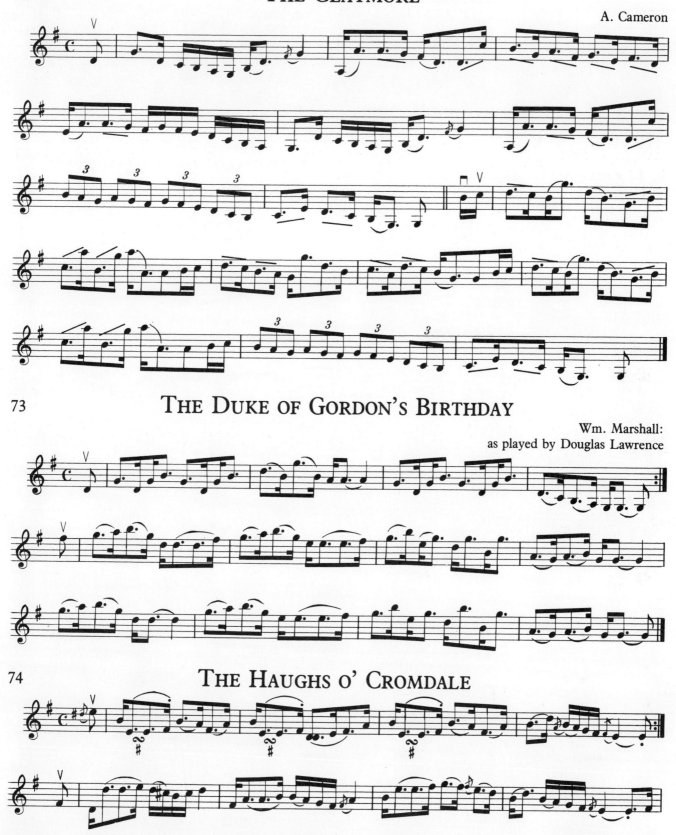

CROPIE'S STRATHSPEY

P. Milne

HEILAN DONALD KISSED KITTY

GARTHLANDS

Jas. MacDonald

78   LADY ANN HOPE

J. Pringle

79   LADY CHARLOTTE CAMPBELL

Nath. Gow

80   THE LAIRD o' MacINTOSH

THE LEYS O' LUNCARTY

81

MR. GORDON OF HALLHEAD

82

Slow

Wm. Marshall

MR. OSWALD OF AUCHINCRUIVE

83

Robt. Mackintosh:
as played by Douglas Lawrence

MONYMUSK

D. Dow

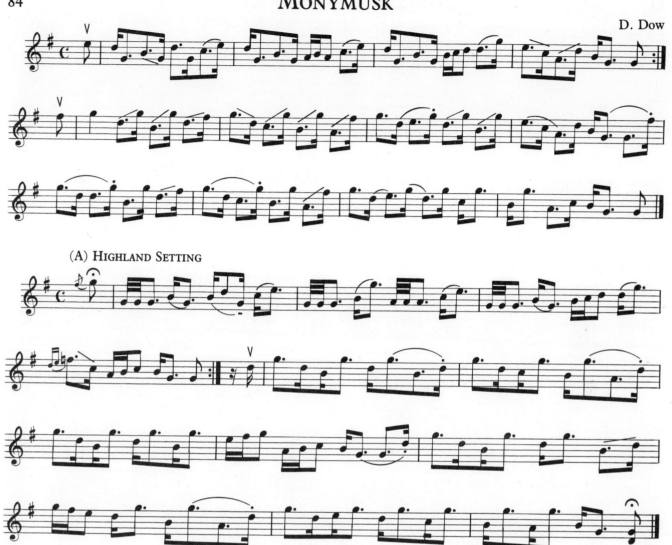

(A) HIGHLAND SETTING

SIR GEORGE CLERK OF PENNYCUICK

Slow

Nath. Gow

TULLOCHGORUM

What need's there be sae great a fraise,
Wi' dringin', dull Italian lays,
I wadna gi'e our ain strathspeys
For half-a-hunder score o' them.
They're dowf and dowie at the best,
Dowf and dowie, dowf and dowie;
Dowf and dowie at the best,
Wi' a' their variorum:
They're dowf and dowie at the best.
Their *allegros* and a' the rest;
They canna please a Scottish taste
Compared wi' Tullochgorum.

REV. J. SKINNER

WHISTLE O'ER THE LAVE O'T

Slowish

Attr. J. Bruce

THE AULD TOON o' AYR

88

BETTY WASHINGTON

89

J. S. Skinner

THE BRAES o' MAR

90

Attr. John Coutts of Deeside

THE BRIDGE OF DEE

J. Young

91

BROCHAN LOM

92

CAMERON'S GOT HIS WIFE AGAIN

93

94

CLACHNACUDDIN

95

CRAIGELLACHIE BRIG

Wm. Marshall

DUNNOTTAR CASTLE

Slow

THE FORTH BRIDGE

W. Blyth

FERINTOSH WHISKY

HUNTLY LODGE

Slow

Nath. Gow

EFFIE GLASGOW OF LONGMORN

Wm. MacPherson

JESSIE SMITH

102 JOHNNIE STEELE

J. Barnett

103 BELLADRUM HOUSE

As played by Angus Cameron

104 THE MARQUIS OF HUNTLY'S HIGHLAND FLING

G. Jenkins

THE KIRRIE KEBBUCK

J. S. Skinner

LADY MARY RAMSAY

Slowish

Nath. Gow

ossia:

LORD LYNDOCH

P. Agnew

THE MARQUIS OF TWEEDALE'S FAVOURITE

D. MacDonald

McKENZIE HAY

J. S. Skinner

MRS. STEWART NICHOLSON

Nath. Gow

Slow

THE MILLER O' HIRN

J. S. Skinner

THE SMITH'S A GALLANT FIREMAN

As played by Bill Hardie

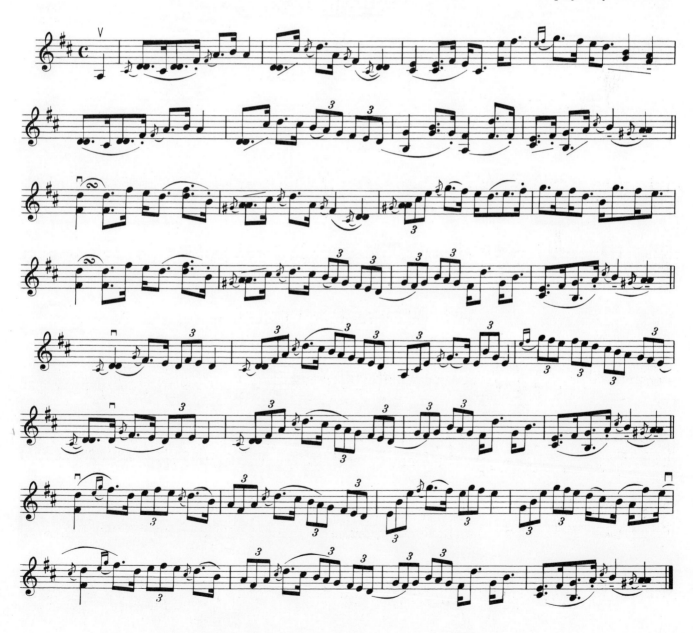

MRS. McINROY OF LUDE

Joseph Lowe: arr. J. M. Hunter

STIRLING CASTLE

Prof. Bannatyne:
as played by Bill Hardie

CARRON WATER

CAPTAIN GILLAN

Wm. Christie

The Bob of Dowally

Arr. J. M. Hunter

118 Because He Was A Bonnie Lad

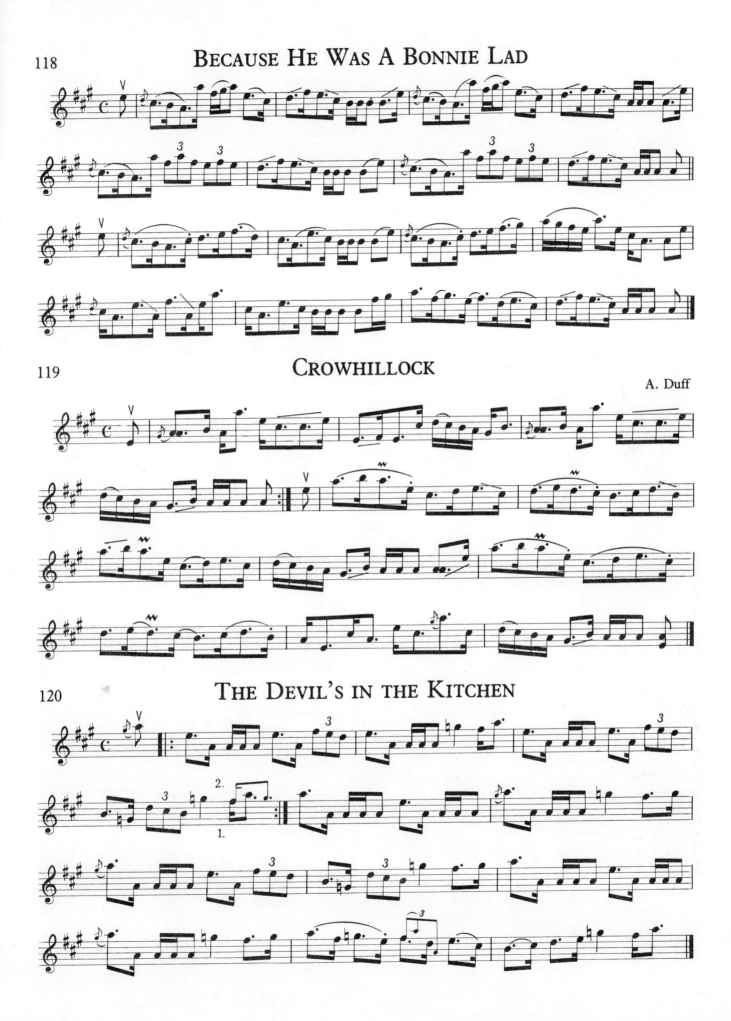

119 Crowhillock

A. Duff

120 The Devil's in the Kitchen

THE COUNTESS OF CRAWFORD
[DUNECHT HOUSE]

Slow

P. Milne:
as played by Arthur S. Robertson

EARL GREY

J. Hill

Forbes Morrison

123

J. S. Skinner

Gille-Callum

124

Glen Grant

125

C. Grant

GLENGRANT

J. S. Skinner: arr. J. M. Hunter

HIGHLAND WHISKY

Niel Gow

THE IRON MAN
[W. M. F. McHardy, Forgue]

J. S. Skinner

J. F. DICKIE'S DELIGHT

J. M. Henderson

Slow

LADY CHARLOTTE BRUCE

Wm. Shepherd

THE LAIRD o' THRUMS

J. S. Skinner

GLENLIVET [WHISKY]
[MINMORE SCHOTTISCHE]

J. S. Skinner

LADY MADELINA SINCLAIR

Wm. Marshall

THE LAIRD o' DRUMBLAIR

J. S. Skinner:
as played by Bill Hardie

LINK HIM DODIE

MADAM FREDERICK

Wm. Marshall

Slow

THE MARCHIONESS OF HUNTLY

Wm. Marshall

Slowish

THE MARCHIONESS OF HUNTLY
[ABOYNE CASTLE]

P. Milne

139

MAGGIE CAMERON

As played by Arthur S. Robertson

140

THE MILLER OF CAMSERNEY

Archie Menzies

141 THE MARQUIS OF HUNTLY'S FAREWELL

Wm. Marshall

142 MISS HALDANE OF GLENEAGLES

143 MISS STEWART OF GRANTULLY

Niel Gow

THE MILLER OF DRONE

As played by Bill Hardie

MISS MAULE

Robt. Mackintosh

MRS. HOOD

Abr. Mackintosh

147 MISS ADMIRAL GORDON

Wm. Marshall

148 MRS. McKENZIE OF APPLECROSS

Joseph Lowe

149 SOUTH OF THE GRAMPIANS

Jas. Porteous:
as played by Bill Hardie

STUMPIE

150

THE THORN BUSH

151

Jas. Fraser

TULCHAN LODGE

152

J. S. Skinner

153

THE WAG O' THE KILT

March-Strathspey

McKenzie Murdoch

154

MR. WILLIAM DAVIDSON

Joseph Lowe

155

MAR CASTLE

Slow

J. S. Skinner

156

J. O. FORBES OF CORSE

P. Milne

Slow

157

BRAIGH BHANBH: THE HIGHLANDS OF BANFFSHIRE

158

THE DUCHESS OF ATHOLE'S SLIPPER

Niel Gow

LORD MOIRA

159

Fine

Dal Segno al Fine

HON. MISS ELLIOT

160

Slow

J. Pringle

MISS CLEMENTINA LOUGHNAN

161 Slow

Nath. Gow

MISS FARQUHARSON OF INVERCAULD

162

Wm. Marshall

MRS. RUSSELL OF BLACKHALL

163

Robt. Mackintosh

BRUACHAN LOCH NIS: THE BANKS OF LOCH NESS

164 Slow

MRS. GARDEN OF TROUP

R. Petrie: arr. J. M. Hunter

BRECHIN CASTLE

THE BRAES O' TULLYMET

THE DUCHESS OF BUCCLEUGH'S FAVOURITE

Slow

THE EWIE WITH THE CROOKED HORN

KINRARA

Wm. Marshall

LADY BOSWELL OF AUCHINLECK

Slow

Nath. Gow

MACKWORTH

Slow

J. S. Skinner: arr. J. M. Hunter

173

LADY CHARLOTTE CAMPBELL

Slow

Robt. Mackintosh

174

THE MARQUIS OF HUNTLY

Wm. Marshall

175

MASTER FRANCIS SITWELL

Slowish

Nath. Gow

MRS. COLQUHOUN GRANT

I. Cooper

MRS. MENZIES OF CULDARE

A. Duff

177

Slow

SPRINGFIELD

Abr. Mackintosh

178

MAISE AN TAOBH TUATH:
THE BEAUTY OF THE NORTH

Capt. S. Fraser

179

Slow

Culloden House

J. Anderson

180

The Dean Brig o' Edinburgh

Airchie Allan

181

The Glories of 'The Star'

J. S. Skinner

182

THE MARCHIONESS OF CORNWALLIS

183

Slow

Wm. Marshall

MISS COXE

184

Slowish

Mrs. McIntyre

SIR JAMES GRANT

185

Slow

J. Anderson

186

CABER FEIDH: THE DEER'S ANTLERS

187

HON. MRS. CAMPBELL OF LOCHNELL

Robt. Mackintosh

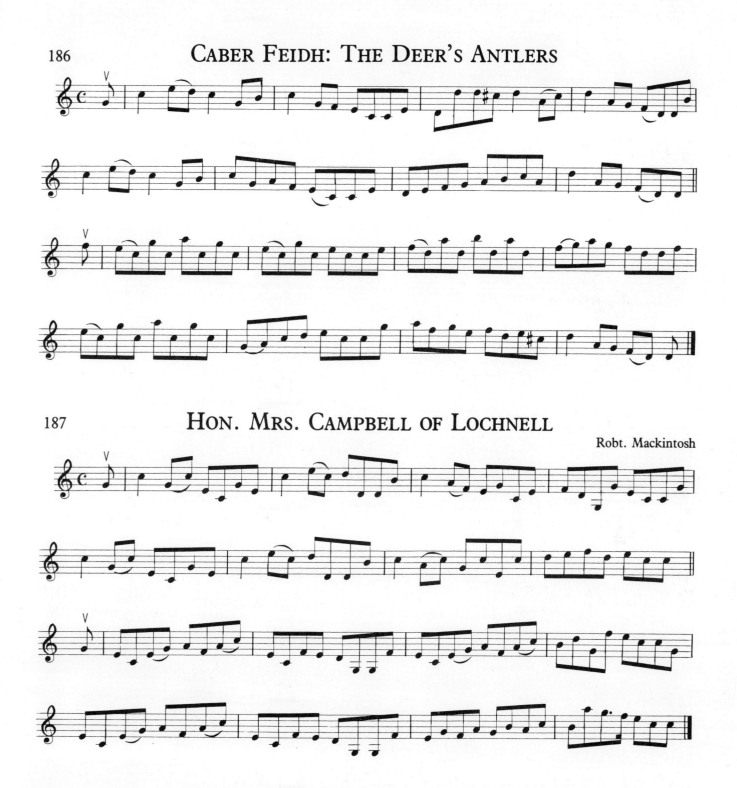

188 BROWN'S REEL

189 JOHN O' GROAT'S HOUSE

190 MRS. DUNDAS OF ARNISTON

Wm. Gow

MISS LYALL

As played by Angus Cameron

MISS SHEPHERD

J. S. Skinner

MUILEANN DUBH: THE BLACK MILL

194   Aandowin at the Bow

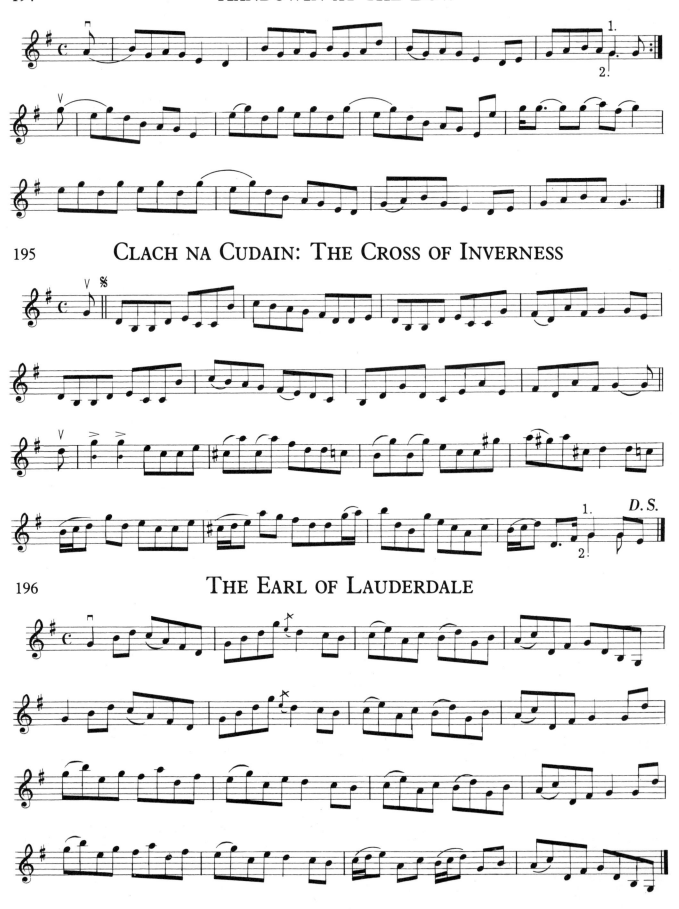

195   Clach na Cudain: The Cross of Inverness

196   The Earl of Lauderdale

JACK IS YET ALIVE

LOCH EARN

Nath. Gow

LOCHRYNACH

200 LORD MACDONALD

201 LORD ELCHO

Robt. Mackintosh

202 MISS BARSTOW

Robt. Mackintosh

203 MISS DOUGLAS MONCRIEFF

Robt. Mackintosh:
as played by Douglas Lawrence

204 TORRYBURN LASSES

205 THE AULD WHEEL
[MILL O' HIRN, CRATHES]

J. S. Skinner

D.S.

1.

2.

206
THE BRIDE'S REEL
[MRS SCOTT SKINNER]

J. S. Skinner

207
THE BRIDGE OF DEE

J. Young

208
THE BRIDGE OF TILT

As played by Angus Cameron

DALKEITH HOUSE

Jas. MacDonald

209

DEIL STICK DA MINISTER

210

DONALD BLUE

211

DA FORFEIT O' DA SHIP

212

THE FORTH BRIDGE

W. Blyth

213

PRETTY PEGGY

214

RACHEL RAE

John Lowe

215

216

Jenny Dang The Weaver

217

Da Mirrie Boys o' Greenland

218

Miss Susan Cooper

R. Cooper

LARGO'S FAIRY DANCE

Nath. Gow: arr. J. M. Hunter

Violin

Piano

Vars.

SLEEPY MAGGIE

Arr. J. M. Hunter

TASTE DA GREEN

THE SPEY IN SPATE

J. S. Skinner

222

THE WIND THAT SHAKES THE BARLEY

223

ANGUS CAMPBELL [GLASGOW]

J. S. Skinner

224

225

BONNIE BANCHORY

J. S. Skinner

226

BRANDLINGS

Abr. Mackintosh

227

THE EARL OF CRAWFORD

P. Milne

228

THE BUNGALOW

J. S. Skinner

229

THE DEIL AMANG THE TAILORS

230

GILLAN'S REEL

P. Milne

2.

1.

D. S.

Da Tushkar

R. Cooper

[A. A.] Gladstone [Edinburgh]

J. S. Skinner

DUNTROON CASTLE

Bagpipe Reel

As played by Arthur S. Robertson

THE HIGH ROAD TO LINTON

THE EARL OF ERROL

F. Peacock

THE HURDLE RACE

Jas. Fraser

JOHN McNEIL

P. Milne

238 INVER LASSES

239 JAMES F. DICKIE

J. M. Henderson

240 THE LEFT-HANDED FIDDLER

J. S. Skinner

KATE DALRYMPLE

Arr. J. M. Hunter

242

LADY DOLL SINCLAIR

243

THE MARQUIS OF HUNTLY

P. Milne:
as played by Arthur S. Robertson

244

THE MARQUIS OF TULLYBARDINE

John Crerar

THE MASON'S APRON

245

THE MILL BURN

246

Jas. Fraser

THE PERTH [SHIRE] HUNT

247

Miss Stirling

248

MISS WEDDERBURN

249

MRS. MCLEOD OF RAASAY

250

REEL OF TULLOCH

The St. Kilda Wedding

251

Sheep Shanks

252

Sir Reginald MacDonald

253

The Stuart's Rant

254

THE £10 FIDDLE

255

J. S. Skinner

THE WAVERLEY BALL

256

Joseph Lowe

Timour the Tartar

Arr. J. M. Hunter

FRANK GILRUTH

P. Milne

ARCHIE MENZIES

John Lowe

CARNIE'S CANTER

J. S. Skinner

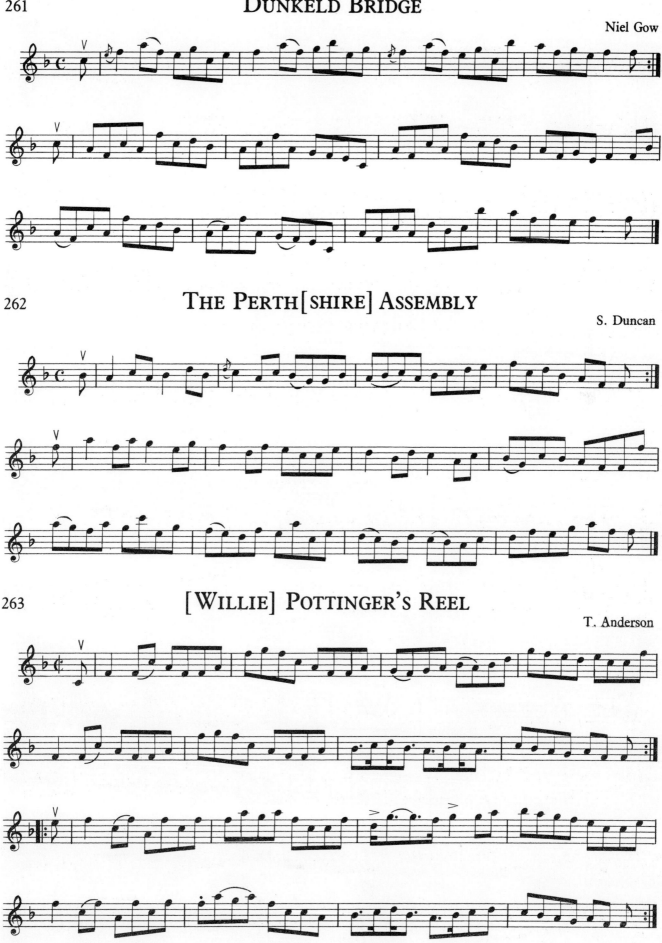

261

DUNKELD BRIDGE

Niel Gow

262

THE PERTH[SHIRE] ASSEMBLY

S. Duncan

263

[WILLIE] POTTINGER'S REEL

T. Anderson

THE COUNTESS OF SUTHERLAND

G. Jenkins

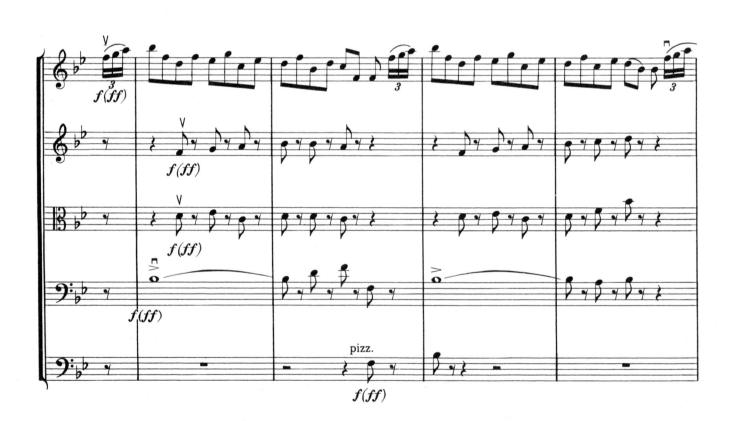

265

COLONEL McBAIN

266

CAPTAIN KEELER

LADY CHARLOTTE CAMPBELL

Robt. Mackintosh: arr. J. M. Hunter

LADY MONTGOMERIE

Lord Eglintoun

MISS MARY WALKER [OF PETERHEAD]

J. S. Skinner

MISS CAMERON OF BALVENIE

Wm. Marshall

271 **Miss Dumbreck**

272 **Miss Elenora Robertson**

Robt. Mackintosh

273 **Miss Loudon**

Robt. Lowe

274 **Miss Margaret Graham of Gartmore's Favourite**

Wm. Marshall

275 **Mrs. Fraser of Cullen**

Wm. Marshall

276 **Geordie Affleck**

277
Miss Gordon of Gight

I. Cooper

278
Mrs. McPherson of Gibton

Wm. Marshall

279
Nuaghalachd: The Novelty

Capt. S. Fraser

JIGS

DRUMMOND CASTLE

280

THE NEW-RIGGED SHIP
[MISS FINLAY'S DELIGHT]

281

282

TAM'S HUNTING HORN

I. Munro

283

DUMFRIES HOUSE

J. Riddell

284

DROPS OF BRANDY

THE HAYMAKERS

285

HAMILTON HOUSE

286

MIDDLING, THANK YOU

287

288
DA FOULA REEL

289
MISS HANNAH OF ELGIN

Wm. Marshall

290
ANDREW CARR

DOWN THE TANNOCH ROAD

A. Harper

THE LASSIES O' DUNSE

MISS SALLY HUNTER OF THURSTON

Nath. Gow

MISS STEWART OF BOMBAY

Wm. Marshall

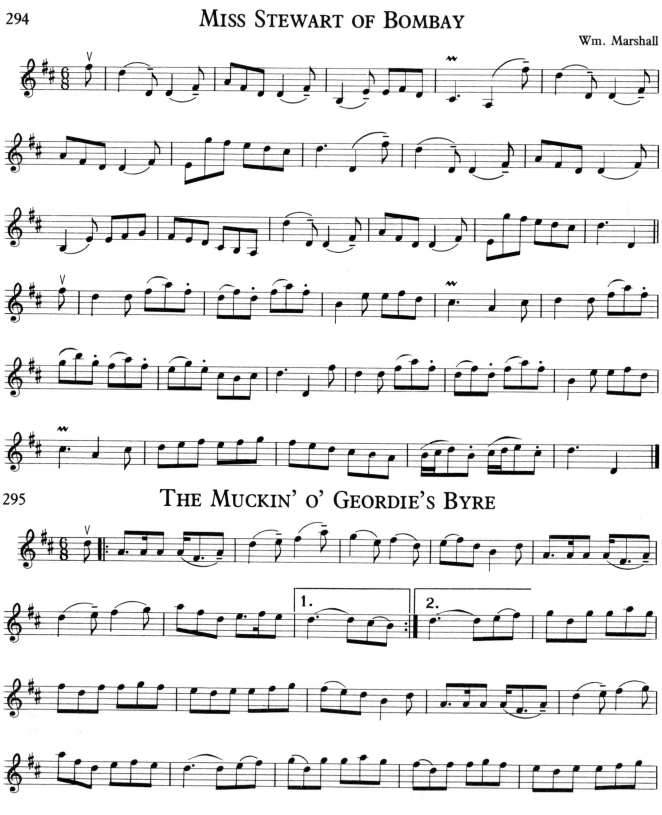

295 THE MUCKIN' O' GEORDIE'S BYRE

296 THE DEUKS DANG O'ER MY DADDIE

297 PETER'S PEERIE BOAT

T. Anderson

298 LAMB SKINNET

299

THE COCK O' THE NORTH

300

MISS STEWART'S FANCY

Abr. Mackintosh

301

NEWCASTLE BRIDGE

Abr. Mackintosh

RATTLIN' ROARIN' WILLIE

THE STOOL OF REPENTANCE

Niel Gow

TEVIOT BRIG

305

BALCOMIE HOUSE

306

LIGHT AND AIRY

307

MISS ANN CAMERON OF BALVENIE

Wm. Marshall

Country Dances and Scots Measures

308

The Cairdin' O't

309

The East Neuk o' Fife

THE FLOWERS OF EDINBURGH

310

311

THE MARCHFIELD BRAE SCOTS MEASURE

R. Gonnella

312

MISS CATHERINE MAXWELL'S SCOTS MEASURE

Abr. Mackintosh

THE WHITE COCKADE

313

STATEN ISLAND

314

MEG MERRILEES

315

ROXBURGH CASTLE

316

THE SOLDIERS JOY

317

SPEED THE PLOUGH

318

THE TRIUMPH

THE DASHING WHITE SERGEANT

321

JOHNNIE IN NETHER MAINS

Niel Gow

322

MISS ANDY CAMPBELL'S SCOTS MEASURE

A. McGlashan

323

PETRONELLA

LADY MARY HAY'S SCOTS MEASURE

HORNPIPES

325   ## THE NEWCASTLE HORNPIPE

J. Hill

326   ## THE TRUMPET HORNPIPE

or

LOCH LEVEN CASTLE

THE RIGHTS OF MAN

HARVEST HOME

Arr. J. M. Hunter

330

MISS GAYTON

331

THE LOCHMABEN HORNPIPE

332

THE MATHEMATICIAN

J. S. Skinner

THE HAWK HORNPIPE

J. Hill: arr. J. M. Hunter

334

THE BOW-LEGGED BOSUN

J. M. Hunter

335

ADMIRAL NELSON

Niel Gow

336

THE COLLEGE HORNPIPE

THE BEE'S WING HORNPIPE

J. Hill

THE HIGH LEVEL HORNPIPE

J. Hill

Fine

D. S. al Fine

THE SECOND STAR HORNPIPE

G. Tate: arr. with variations
by Arthur S. Robertson

BANKS HORNPIPE

340

Parazotti

MARCHES

341 DELTING BRIDAL MARCH

342 EIRIDH NA FINNACHA' GAELACH:
THE REBEL WAR SONG

343 THE BARREN ROCKS OF ADEN

A. MacKellar

DA GUISERS' MARCH

G. Stove

345 ## SCOTT SKINNER'S COMPLIMENTS TO DR McDONALD

J. S. Skinner

THE ATHOLE HIGHLANDERS' FAREWELL
TO LOCH KATRINE

W. Rose

THE CAMERON HIGHLANDERS

J. S. Skinner

QUEEN ELIZABETH MARCH

J. Moir

McLean of Pennycross

A. Ferguson:
as played by Arthur S. Robertson

MANGISTER VOE

T. Anderson

MR. MICHIE

351

A. Fitchet

THE ATHOLE VOLUNTEERS MARCH

Niel Gow

McGregor's Freedom March

I. Munro

MISCELLANEOUS

ORANGE AND BLUE

Highland Schottische

As played by Bill Hardie

THE HEN'S MARCH O'ER THE MIDDEN

With Humour

QUICKSTEP

Niel Gow: vars. by J. M. Hunter

MORMOND BRAES

Bothy Ballad

THE LOVAT SCOUTS

Quickstep

J. S. Skinner

359

THE BONNIE LASS O' FYVIE

Bothy Ballad

360   HON. CAPT. ELLIOT'S QUICKSTEP

J. Pringle

361   THE PETERHEAD POLKA

D.C. al Fine

CAMPBELL'S POLKA

J. M. Hunter

Fine

D.C. al Fine

THE BARNYARDS OF DELGATY

Bothy Ballad

McFarlane o' the Sproats o' Burnieboozie

W. Kemp

Bothy Ballad

365

Aith Rant

Trowie Tune

HISTORICAL AND OTHER NOTES

1
Printed in Gow's second collection with the alternative title *Miss Duff's Fancy*.

2
Lucy Johnston of Hilton (1765–1797) was one of a number of aristocratic amateur composers of the late eighteenth century. A noted belle of the Edinburgh Dance Assembly, she was much admired by the Gows, Burns and Robert Mackintosh, who dedicated his second collection to her.

3
A very beautiful Gaelic air. Captain Simon Fraser, in his 1816 Collection, printed the Gs in bars 4, 12 and 20 as G sharp, thus robbing the air of much of its simplicity and modal character.

5
Coilsfield was the home of Colonel Hugh Montgomerie (1749–1819), twelfth Earl of Eglinton, an enthusiast for Scottish dance music. He was the dedicatee of Gow's fourth collection.

7
The Rev. Archie Beaton was Minister of Dundonald Parish Church, Ayrshire. A champion of Gaelic culture, he died suddenly while acting as President of An Comunn Gaidhealach at the Stirling Mod in 1971. The air was written by John Mason, a native of the Orkney Islands now practising law in Troon. He is conductor of the Kilmarnock and Ayr Strathspey and Reel Society, and a well-known conductor at Fiddle Rallies.

8
A *pièce de résistance* of Scottish fiddlers—yet it was written by an Englishman, the Rev. William Leeves (1748–1828), rector of Wrington in Somerset, to words by Lady Anne Barnard (née Lindsay). The words were originally set to a fine old Scottish air, *The Bridegroom Grat*.

9
One of the finest elegiac airs in the repertoire, written by Gow on the death of his friend and benefactor, 'Auld Abercarney'.

10
This famous rant was composed by the notorious James Macpherson (1675–1700), freebooter and fiddler, in the final hours before his execution at the Market Cross of Banff on 16 November 1700. Macpherson is reputed to have played the air at the scaffold, then offered his fiddle to anyone in the crowd. No one dared to accept it for fear of being implicated, so he smashed it over his knee and threw the pieces to the crowd. The remains of the fiddle are now in the Macpherson Clan Museum at Newtonmore.

12
Arthur Scott Robertson (1911–) was the winner of the famous BBC fiddle competition held in Perth in 1969. A native of Bressay, he spent his working life in Lerwick as a manager in an oil distribution firm. The air is dedicated to his wife.

13
This excellent air was composed by the Rev. William McLeod as he sailed from his native Bracadale in the Isle of Skye to take up a parish in Argyllshire.

15
A tribute by the famous collector Captain Simon Fraser of Knockie (1773–1852) to 'Famous Niel'. Fraser was born at Ardachie near Fort Augustus. Captain Macdiarmid, a contemporary violinist, said of Fraser's playing: 'I never heard anyone make the fiddle *speak Gaelic* so beautifully.'

17
A well-loved air by the late Charlie Hunter of Oban, a radio operator on the MacBrayne steamers which ply the west-coast routes.

18
John Glen regarded this air as a plagiarism of Marshall's *Miss Admiral Gordon*. The reader can judge for himself by comparing this air with No. 147. Burns distinguished between the two, and used both as song airs.

19
Niel's second wife was Margaret Urquhart of Perth, whose death after thirty years of happy marriage inspired this splendid melody.

20
An air by Scott Skinner to his first wife Jane Stuart of Aberlour, who died suddenly after twelve years of marriage.

21
Skinner wrote this air, the most popular of his compositions during his own lifetime, after meeting a servant girl called Wilhelmina Bell (later Mrs. Peters) at a house party in Union Terrace, Aberdeen, in December 1884.

23
Peter Milne (1824–1908) was one of Scott Skinner's teachers. A native of Kincardine O' Neil, he lived most of his early years in Tarland, where he worked as a farm boy. He was a self-taught fiddler and earned his living playing in theatres throughout the country. Later he became an opium addict, and in company with the blind musician Willie Grant he earned a living playing on the ferry-boats crossing the Forth. He was a talented composer and a natural fiddler who, in his own words, 'was that fond o' my fiddle, I could sit inside it and look oot'. He died in Aberdeen after a long illness.

25
A haunting air which Skinner was inspired to compose after watching a young mother care for her sick child in a Forres hotel room.

26
Originally a strathspey in C, this old air by Crockat has achieved great popularity in this arrangement by Scott Skinner.

27
A pibroch-style air commemorating the famous heights in India (taken by the Gordon Highlanders in 1897) where Piper Findlater won his Victoria Cross.

28
> 'The flo'ers grow fair on the lowland vale,
> an' green grow the wids on the braes,
> an' saft an' low sing the scented gales
> in the lang, lang simmer days;
> But dearer to me are the mountains blue
> where grow the heath an' fern,
> an' the bonniest flo'er is the ane I lo'e

30 that blooms 'mang the braes o' the Quern.'
To the memory of Piper Willie McLennan of Edinburgh who tragically died while touring America with Skinner in 1893.

31
Neil Gow Jnr. was the first son of Nathaniel Gow. A keen amateur musician, he entered the medical profession and subsequently joined his father in a music publishing business. He died in 1823 aged twenty-eight.

32
George MacIlwham is a flautist with the BBC Scottish Symphony Orchestra. He is also a piper of some repute, and has written a number of orchestral pieces which are strongly influenced, especially melodically, by his deep interest in traditional music.

33
Charles Grant, M.A. (1807–1892) was a schoolmaster at Aberlour. He composed some fifty-six tunes, mostly strathspeys and reels. Grant was a pupil of Marshall's, and played Marshall's favourite strathspeys to him on his deathbed. His family bequeathed Marshall's violin to Grant in 1851.

34
Frank Ronald Jamieson was born in Vidlin in 1919. He was secretary and office manager to a weaving and knitting company in Lerwick. He wrote this splendid air in 1965 in memory of his favourite sister with whom he lived for many years until her sudden death.

39
One of the best examples of the extensive use of variations prevalent in the eighteenth century, showing the influence of the Italianate on folk music.

41
Angus Cameron, a mathematics teacher in Kirriemuir, is the son of the late Will Cameron, a well-known exponent of Scottish fiddle music and a member of the famous Cameron

family—all of whom were fiddle pupils of 'Dancie' Reid of Newtyle. The late Alex Webster was a native of Edzell, and while working as a gamekeeper at Glenbucket in Strathdon he became intensely interested in fiddle-making and made some fine instruments. He donated one of his fiddles to Angus Cameron, hence *Angus Cameron's Compliments*.

44
Originally called (by Marshall) *Miss Dallas*, this tune was plagiarised by Niel Gow, who lowered the key from G to F, added a distinctive last cadence, and renamed it *The Royal Gift* or *The Marquis of Huntly's Snuff Mill*, under which name it has enjoyed great popularity.

46
An air to celebrate the departure of the Duke of Gordon's third daughter, Susan, who married the Duke of Manchester in 1793. Niel Gow, in his fifth Collection, 're-christened' the tune *Honest Men and Bonnie Lassies*.

47
The tune alludes to the prohibition of whisky distilling in 1799. 'A Highlander's farewell to his favourite beverage', as Niel Gow put it.

50
The Duchess was Georgina, fifth and youngest daughter of the fourth Duke of Gordon, who married the Duke of Bedford.

51
Captain Simon Fraser relates the story behind this air as follows: 'Prince Charles is known to have sustained extreme hardship in wandering on his way from the place of his defeat to the Isle of Skye, often remaining all night, in the cold month of April, in the open air, without approaching house or cabin. He sent one of his attendants to entreat for quarters. From the hesitation and impatience of this individual, anxious yet afraid to communicate his request to the goodwife, in case of speedy pursuit; the air at first represents him as scarcely whispering his request, in broken sentences, but, on finding they were likely to be well received, he acquires more confidence, and the second part seems to picture a composure, however temporary, at their success.'

52
One of the houses of the Gordon family.

53
This fine air relates to a supposed utterance of Prince Charlie on the night after his defeat at Culloden. In hiding and ultra-suspicious, he mistook the terrified whispers of the little girls of the house for the voices of betrayal. On discovering his mistake, he exclaimed, 'Hard is my fate, when the innocent prattle of children could annoy me so much.'

58
It is difficult to say for certain who wrote this fine tune. A variant of it was called *Miss Joan Kier* in its earliest printed source—John Clarkson's Musical Entertainment, London, c.1796. Another appears in T. Calvert's Collection c.1799 as *Sir Hendry's Strathspey*. Nath. Gow printed it in 1800 under its present title but it also has a strong affinity with Marshall's *Invereshie*.

59
An old air from the Knockie Collection 'complimentary to the family of Col. Rose of Kilravock—one of the most ancient and respected families in the north.'

60
James Henry (1860–1914) was born in Garmond, Aberdeenshire. He was leader of the Aberdeen Strathspey and Reel Society from its inception in 1903 until his death. The Auld Brig o' Balgownie which spans the River Don was erected in the thirteenth and fourteenth centuries, and has a magnificent Gothic arch sixty-seven feet in span, resting on rocks on either side.

62
This air was wrongly ascribed to James Oswald (1711–1769) but he never claimed it. The words of the song were written by Richard Hewitt of Cumberland, who acted as amanuensis to the Scottish lyric poet Dr. Blacklock (1721–1791). Roslin Castle is a fourteenth-century castle in Midlothian which possesses a magnificent, small chapel founded in 1446 by the Earl of Orkney and Roslin.

63
The Marchioness of Huntly, Elizabeth Brodie (1794–1864), who had married the future fifth Duke of Gordon in 1813, was the dedicatee of Marshall's 1821 Collection, even though her tastes were more for psalms and hymn tunes than strathspeys and reels.

64
Above the Falls of Kilmorack on the river Beauly is the Pass of Dhreim. Skinner visited it with his two great friends Donald Morrison and Dr. McDonald. Morrison told Skinner how some time previously a traction engine with a couple of trucks had fallen one hundred feet from the road into the gorge, killing two men. A strange phenomenon happened—most of the birches within thirty yards of the accident began to wither away. Skinner became obsessed with the tragedy and gave it expression through this fine melody.

67
A development of the fine old strathspey named after Mrs. Grant of Laggan (1775–1838).

68
This tune is claimed by Niel Gow in his third Collection, but Malcolm McDonald also claimed it, and published it as *Miss Sarah Drummond of Perth*.

72
The strathspey was named after the steamer *Claymore* which sails to the Hebrides out of Oban.

73
Douglas Lawrence hails from Buckie and is Hector MacAndrew's most distinguished pupil. Although still only in his early twenties and a student at the Royal Scottish Academy of Music, he has already won every major fiddle competition.

77
James MacDonald was a contemporary of Niel Gow. Like Gow he earned his living playing and composing.

78
First published in John Pringle's first Collection (1800) as *Miss Hope's Strathspey*, in the key of D. Gow published it in G and added triplets to the second measure. John Pringle was a Border fiddler chosen by Lord Minto to lead his band when he was Governor General of India.

84
Daniel Dow (1732–1783), born in Kirkmichael, Perthshire, worked as a music teacher in Edinburgh. He presented concerts in St. Mary's Hall, Niddry's Wynd, for many years, and is buried in the Canongate Churchyard. The full title of this, his most famous composition, was *Sir Archibald Grant of Monemusk's Reel*.

86
The Rev. John Skinner (1721–1807) was pastor of the Episcopal Chapel at Langside, near Peterhead. His celebrated song came to the defence of Scottish folk music at a time when Italian music and musicians were finding great favour with the middle and upper classes in Scotland. Other poets rallied to the cause, e.g. Robert Burns in his satirical political song 'Amang the trees' and Robert Fergusson in his poem 'Daft Days'.

87
This air is attributed to John Bruce, 'a red-wud Highlandman' as Burns described him. He was born in Braemar, and spent some time as a prisoner in Edinburgh Castle for being out in the 1745 Rising. He later lived in Dumfries and died there in 1785.

89
A tune that has recently come to light and is published here for the first time. Betty Washington was a music hall artist.

91
James Young (1815–1851) was born in Montrose. In 1837 he moved to Aberdeen to work as a teacher and leader of the orchestra in the Theatre Royal, Marischal Street.

95
Marshall composed this magnificent strathspey, perhaps the finest in the whole repertoire, to celebrate the opening of the bridge over the River Spey at Craigellachie.

96
The ancient ruin of Dunnottar Castle stands on the cliffs a few miles south of Stonehaven. The air is thought to have been composed by either James Young (see 91) or John Gunn (1813–1884) of Peterhead.

97
Williamson Blyth (1821–1897) wrote this strathspey to celebrate the opening in 1890 of the magnificent cantilever bridge designed by Sir Benjamin Baker and built at a cost of £3,200,000.

100

The late Willie MacPherson (1920–1974) was born in Elgin. A brilliant interpreter of slow airs, he was for many years in the first violin section of the Scottish National Orchestra before returning to Elgin to teach and found the local Strathspey and Reel Society. Effie Glasgow—now living in retirement in Plockton—is the wife of Harry Glasgow, the former excise officer at the Longmorn Distillery.

102

James Barnett (1847–1898) of Kirkwall is given the credit for the original setting of this air. However it has been developed by many composers and players since, and is known under many other names, e.g. *The New Brig o' Dee*; *Bob Steele*; *The Miller o' Dervil*; *Benholm Castle*; *The Auld Brig o' Ayr*.

104

George Jenkins was one of the many dancing masters who went to London to teach 'Scotch Dancing'. He died there in 1806.

105

'Kebbuck' is the Scots word for a large whole cheese. When tenants of Skinner's friend Alex McPherson ('The Laird o' Thrums') paid rent he always offered them a whisky, a bannock and a slice of kebbuck.

109

McKenzie Hay was the President of the Caledonian Society of London.

111

'Lad, cam' ye doun by Feugh's green howe,
The Feugh that rins through Crathes, O?
Heard ye a fiddler dirl a bow,
Wi' something like a pathos, O?
Weel, gin he meet wi' your applause,
I brawly can discern, O,
The dusty-noted fiddler was
"The Miller o' the Hirn", O.'

This was Skinner's first composition (and one of his best), a tribute to John Johnston, the old miller whom Skinner often visited as a child. His grandfather and Johnston were married to sisters.

112

William (Bill) J. Hardie has the most distinguished fiddling pedigree of today's players. His great-great-grandfather, Peter Hardie of Dunkeld (1775–1863), was a pupil of Niel Gow. Bill, who works as a violin teacher in Grampian Region, is an acknowledged exponent of bowing technique, and this strathspey and the others he has meticulously set out will repay intensive study.

113

Also known as *Capt. Carrick's Rant*.

116

William Christie (1778–1849) was a dancing master in Cuminestown, Aberdeenshire. He published his Collection in 1820.

119

Archibald Duff published his first Collection in 1794. A native of Montrose, he later moved to Aberdeen to take over the music/dancing-master practice of the celebrated Francis Peacock.

122

James Hill lived in Gateshead. He was a fine composer, especially of hornpipes.

123

Forbes Morrison (1833–1906) was a dancing master in Tarves. He was an expert in the use of the short snap bow and syncopated triplets.

124

This is the tune used for the Highland Sword Dance.

126

Unlike the previous tune, which celebrates the district, Skinner's tune is dedicated to James Grant of Glengrant.

128

See note to No. 134.

129

James F. Dickie was born in Old Deer in 1886 and moved to New Deer where he spent most of his life. Although not well known outside his native Buchan, he was a 'weel-kent and respected player' there for well over fifty years. His particular forte was playing his own florid variations to many of the famous tunes. Now over ninety, he lives quietly in Stonehaven.

130

William Shepherd was Nathaniel Gow's partner in the music-publishing business in Edinburgh. He published two collections of his own besides contributing to the Gow collections. He died in 1812.

131

Skinner's nickname for Alex McPherson, coal-merchant and property owner in Kirriemuir. Thrums is the old name for Kirriemuir.

134

William F. McHardy of Drumblair was a friend and benefactor of Skinner's. He made a fortune of £100,000 in engineering enterprises in South America before returning to live at Forgue near Huntly.

136

Madam Frederick was a famous dancer who often entertained at Gordon Castle. Her favourite tune for dancing to was Marshall's slow strathspey *The Recovery*. Marshall later changed the title in her honour.

137

The wife of the fifth Duke of Gordon (see note 63).

139

One of the fiddle 'arrangements' of pipe music for which Arthur Robertson has become justly famous. This and Nos. 233 and 349 will repay great study, as they show in detail what can be achieved in terms of bowing, particularly the transference of pipe grace-notes to the fiddle.

141

Marshall wrote this air to commemorate the departure of the young Marquis on 'his continental tour' or, more likely, when he set off with the Gordon Highlanders in 1799 to the Helder. Marshall in the first part of the tune attempted to imitate the wailing of the parents and in the second part the crying of the children.

146

Abraham Mackintosh (born 1769) was the second son of 'Red Rob'. He was also a fiddle player and dancing master, first in Edinburgh and then in Newcastle. He published three short volumes of his own music.

147

Margaret Gordon, daughter of Admiral William Gordon, was the dedicatee of this fine strathspey, to which Burns set one of his best-known songs—'Of a' the airts the wind can blaw'.

148

Joseph Lowe (1797–1866) from Marykirk was the editor of the famous Lowe's Collection of 1844.

149

James Porteous (1762–1847) of Meinfoot, Ecclefechan, was one of the famous Border fiddlers of the early nineteenth century.

152

Tulchan Lodge, Advie, was where Skinner taught dancing to the family of Lady Chetwode of Oakley in his early days as a dancing master.

153

McKenzie Murdoch (1871–1923), the 'Scotch Paganini', hailed from Glasgow. He studied with Herr Sons, the Dutch musician and leader of the Scottish Orchestra, and he toured extensively with his friend Harry Lauder. He was a brilliant violinist, especially in the execution of harmonics, and his playing was characterised by a great sense of 'charm and pathos'. He wrote the famous ballad song 'Hame o' Mine'.

162

This strathspey was originally called by Marshall *Lady Louisa Gordon*. Gow reprinted it under the title *Miss McLeod's Fancy* with no composer's credit. When it appeared in Marshall's posthumous collection it was re-christened *Miss Farquharson of Invercauld*.

165

Robert Petrie (1767–1830), a native of Kirkmichael, was employed at Troup House as a gardener. He was an excellent player who won the 'silver bow' at a competition in Edinburgh in 1822. He published four collections.

166

Brechin Castle is the seat of the Earls of Dalhousie. The tune was known as *Miss Douglas of Brigton* (M. McDonald's 1792 Collection) and *Lady Harriot Hay* (Petrie's second Collection, 1795) before Gow published it under the present title in his first

Repository (1799).

167
Robert Petrie is sometimes accredited as being the composer of this fine strathspey, but he never claimed it. Aliases include *Knit the Pocky*; *D. Dick's Favourite*; *Mrs. Grant of Grant*; *Birnieboozle*.

169
The title is a euphemistic synonym for 'the whisky still with its crooked—or rather, spiral—apparatus'.

170
Kinrara was the summer residence of the wife of the fourth Duke of Gordon. Gow printed this tune under the title *The Countess of Dalkeith* in his fourth Collection.

176
Isaac Cooper (c.1755–1820) was a music and dancing teacher in Banff. He published two collections of his own music. The arrangement printed here is from his own manuscripts.

180
First printed in Morrison's Highland Collection (1812). Exactly who J. Anderson is is not known. Could he be the John Anderson who himself published a collection of Highland Strathspeys c.1789, or is he the Anderson who, in association with Johnson the Edinburgh engraver, was responsible for the preparatory work for Morrison's Collection?

181
Airchie Allan (1794–1837) of Forfar was thought to have been a fiddler in Nath. Gow's band for a time. Alexander Lowson described Allan's playing as 'neat and powerful especially in the Strathspeys'. His cousin James Allan (1800–1877) was also a famous fiddler. The original title of this strathspey was *Miss Gray of Carse*, but it was taken up and played into popularity under its present name by Peter Milne.

182
Dedicated to Mrs. Fraser, Nairn, the proprietor of the 'Star'.

183
Louisa, the fourth daughter of the fourth Duke of Gordon, became Marchioness of Cornwallis through her marriage to Viscount Brome, later to be the Marquis. This slow strathspey was regarded by the Duke as one of Marshall's best melodies. His Grace's signal for the termination of a concert was by calling for it to be played.

184
The composer is one of the many dilettantes—'Ladies resident in the Highlands of Scotland'—who contributed to the Gow Collections.

186
The tune used for the famous Highland Dance of the same name, during which the dancers portray with the arms and fingers the shape of Caber Feidh—the Deer's Antlers.

189
John O'Groats is a village on the north coast of Caithness. Mention of 'John O'Groat's house' is found early in the seventeenth century and the family held lands in Canisbay from the fifteenth century onwards. There were eight families of that name and they met annually to celebrate their arrival with a feast until disputes over precedence arose. These were settled by John O'Groat who built a house with an octagonal room and table so that all were 'head of the table'.

190
William Gow (1751–1791) was Niel Gow's eldest son. A player of 'bold and spirited style', he took over the leadership of the McGlashan band when the 'King' retired.

191
Companion reel to No. 67.

192
Miss Shepherd was an assistant in Strachan's music shop, Belmont Street, Aberdeen, a favourite rendezvous on a Saturday night for fiddlers.

194
This Shetland tune title refers to the action of keeping the boat steady at the marker buoy by 'iddling' with the oars.

195
In Captain Fraser's words: 'This air celebrates the foundation-stone of Inverness, which is still religiously preserved near the cross. It was formerly the resting place of the servant girls, in bringing their water pails from the river, and of course a celebrated rendezvous for obtaining all the news and scandal.'

205
One of the 'birling' reels of which Skinner was so fond. (See Nos. 222, 224, 232, 236, 240, 260, 269.) The birl acts like a little drum roll. It is best executed by playing near the point of the bow and giving a subtle flick of a loose wrist.

207
Companion reel to No. 91.

209
James MacDonald was one of the many 'professional' fiddlers who contributed to the Gow collections.

210
This is a protest tune composed in the days when ministers tried to stop the 'disreputable practice of fiddling'.

213
Companion reel to No. 97.

215
John Lowe was a dancing master in Marykirk. The reel first appeared in Archibald Duff's Collection of 1794 as *Raecheal Rea's Rant*.

216
The Rev. Alexander Garden (1688–1778), minister of Birse, Aberdeenshire, has been credited with this air. The anecdote associated with the air relates that c.1746 the minister's 'handy-man', an ex-weaver from Marywell called Jock, hotly refused to clean the parson's boots when requested to do so by Mrs. Garden. The enraged minister's wife gave him such a beating with her 'tattie-beetle' that he soon performed the task.

219
Composed by Nath. Gow for the Fife Hunt, 1802, this reel has become one of the most popular tunes with fiddlers and dance bands. The variations are based on Scott Skinner's.

221
This reel celebrates the coming of spring when the livestock could once again feed off the grasslands.

225
The birthplace of J. Scott Skinner.

226
Sometimes called *The Fox*.

228
The bungalow in Forgue which the 'Laird o' Drumblair' made available, rent free, to Skinner for several years.

231
Ronnie Cooper hails from Lerwick and is one of the most prolific of today's Shetland composers. A self-taught musician, he learned to play the piano and accordion 'by ear' and is much in demand as an accompanist. He got the idea for 'Da Tushkar' when he was in the local smithy, at that time owned by two of Shetland's best fiddle players—Willie Hunter Senior and Junior. They were busy making a tushkar, which is the tool used in Shetland to cut the peat.

235
The fifteenth Earl of Erroll, to whom this tune is dedicated, lived at Slains and at Delgatie Castle, near Turriff. He was High Constable of Scotland and a great scholar and patron of the arts. Francis Peacock was appointed in 1747 by the Town Council of Aberdeen. He was told he might take '7 shillings sterling monthly from each scholar, besides paying for the music'. Also he was 'to be the sole dancing master within the burgh during his good behaviour'. His behaviour must have been exemplary, because he remained in his office until his death in 1807 at the age of eighty-four.

237
John McNeil was a famous Highland dancer at the turn of the century. The legendary piper Angus MacPherson, who died a few years ago at the age of ninety-nine and who competed against McNeil many times, acknowledged McNeil's greatness in a simple and telling statement: 'Oh aye, he threw a fine leg.'

240
George Taylor of Aberdeen was the left-handed fiddler. His son George was also a left-handed player and, incredibly, played a normally-strung violin.

241
Kate Dalrymple was a noted beauty—Gainsborough painted her portrait. The tune was published in 1750 under the name *The New Highland Laddie*, and it is also known as *Jinglin' Johnnie*. Under its present title it has achieved great fame by

being used for over thirty years as the signature tune of BBC Radio's Scottish Dance Music programmes.

247

Composed by Miss Magdaline Stirling of Ardoch, c.1788. Its opening is one of the best examples of the use of the upstroke beginning to reels.

250

One of the great male Highland dances. It was a particular favourite of Queen Victoria, who first saw it danced at a ball given by the Marquis of Breadalbane at Taymouth Castle. The dancers on that occasion were the Marquis of Abercorn, the Hon. Fox Maule, Cluny Macpherson and Davidson of Tulloch.

258

Frank Gilruth (1853–1915) was born at Sanquhar, Gartly, Aberdeenshire. He was teacher of commerce at Dumfries Academy from 1882 until his death.

261

The last tune to be composed by Niel Gow.

262

Samson Duncan (1767–1837) was born at Kinclaven. A fine exponent, he was musician to the Laird of Aldie at Meiklour House, and often played in the bands of Niel, Nathaniel and John Gow.

263

Tom Anderson was born in 1910 in Eshaness, six miles from Hillswick, a remote corner of the Nor' West Mainland of Shetland. He is a noted authority on and exponent of the Shetland tradition. He spent his working life in insurance, and on retirement from that profession was appointed the first traditional fiddle tutor in the Shetland schools. He was awarded the M.B.E. in 1977.

267

Companion reel to No. 173.

268

Lord Eglintoun, Colonel Hugh Montgomerie (1749–1819)—'Sodger Hugh' as Burns called him—was an M.P. for Ayrshire.

273

Robert Lowe was the brother of Joseph, the editor of the Lowe Collection.

283

John Riddell (1718–1795) was a blind fiddler from Ayr. He was one of the first fiddle composers to compile a collection of his own music (1766).

288

The popular country dance known nowadays as 'The Foula Reel' was originally known as 'Da Shaalds o' Foula' or 'Da Foula Shaalds'. The Foula Reel was another dance altogether (and the time used was Scottish). Although the tune is known, the dance has been lost.

291

Adie Harper is the fiddler/leader of the popular Wick Scottish Dance Band. He is also a skilled ukelele player and a prolific composer. Tannoch is a district four miles out of Wick where Adie went to school.

297

The tune was written for Peter Leith, the pianist in a dance band which Tom Anderson used to lead. 'Peerie' is Shetland dialect for 'small'. At the time, Peter was trying to sell his small boat, and Tom used to complain that he thought more about the boat than about the piano accompaniments—so he wrote a tune about it!

299

The fifth and last Duke of Gordon was nicknamed 'The Cock o' the North'.

303

The Stool of Repentance was a small stool used in the Old Scottish Kirk to exact penance from sinning members of the congregation. To demonstrate their repentance, the 'defaulters', by order of the Kirk Session, had to sit for one or two weeks on the stool which was situated in full view of the congregation. This form of punishment was particularly used for adulterers. See Burns's 'Holy Willie's Prayer'.

308

The earliest copy of this tune is in Margaret Sinkler's Ms. Musick Book (c.1710) where it is called *Queensbury's Scots Measure*. What was a Scots Measure? Was it the name of a dance or a distinctive type of tune? The answer is far from certain. D. G. MacLennan, in his book *Highland and Traditional Dances of Scotland* describes it as 'a pleasing type of dance tune to which was danced a Twosome or Twasome Strathspey, and in this form the Highland Schottische evolved'.

309

First published in James Oswald's *Caledonian Pocket Companion* Bk. 4 (1752) and called *She griped at the greatest on 't*. It was published three years later in McGibbon's third Collection under its present title.

310

An old Scots Measure published in 1750 to the words 'My love was once a bonny lad'. Re-published in 1751 by James Oswald, in his *Caledonian Pocket Companion*, as *The Flower of Edinburgh*—'Flowers' is a later version.

311

Ron Gonnella is a schoolmaster in Crieff. A native of Dundee, he has played with many of the top Scottish dance bands, and as a soloist he has toured extensively in America and Canada. Marchfield Brae is a steepish hill in Dundee.

313

A cockade is a rosette worn on the hat as a badge. The distinctive cockade of the House of Hanover was a rosette of black, therefore the Jacobites adopted white. The earliest version of the tune was published in 1782 and called *The Ranting Highlandman*.

328

Both this tune and No. 329 are of Irish origin.

332

This tune amply demonstrates Skinner's use of chromaticism and his technical mastery of the violin.

337

This tune, together with Nos. 338 and 340 are the most popular fiddle hornpipes played today.

341

Delting is the district on Mainland Shetland between Olna Firth and Dales Voe. It was long the custom at weddings in Shetland for fiddlers to lead the bridal party to and from church.

342

A well-known Gaelic song praising the Highland clans who joined in the rebellion.

344

Gideon Stove was born in North Roe in 1875 and died in Lerwick in 1954. As a young man he was offered a place in the London Philharmonic Orchestra but preferred to remain in Shetland, where he was a much respected musician and teacher. He was also a prolific composer and wrote this fine march for the Up Helly Aa procession which in former years was led by a fiddle band—now by a brass band.

345

Dr. Keith Norman McDonald (1834–1913) was a native of Ord in Skye. He qualified in medicine at Edinburgh University and practised in his native Skye, Lochaber, Edinburgh and Burma. He was an accomplished musician and violinist, and edited the *Gesto Collection of Highland Music* (1895) and the *Skye Collection of Reels and Strathspeys* (1897).

347

The regiment in which the composer's brother Sandy served for eleven years. Sandy was a dancing master who enjoyed the patronage of Sir Charles Forbes of New Strathdon.

348

Jimmy Moir was born in Ferryden near Montrose. He moved to Glasgow to join the police and rose to the rank of sergeant. He joined the Glasgow Strathspey and Reel Society in 1926, and in 1954 succeeded Sinclair Rae as conductor. For the past few years he has been organiser and conductor of the Daily Record Golden Fiddle Rallies, and in 1979 was awarded the M.B.E. for his services to fiddle music. He wrote this march in 1977 to commemorate the Queen's Silver Jubilee.

350

A 'voe' is the Shetland name for a sea inlet.

351

John D. Michie was the owner of the music shop in Brechin. After losing the power of some fingers in the 1914–18 war he gave up playing and became an expert fiddle repairer. Angus Fitchet was born in Dundee in 1910. He has played the fiddle

in many leading country dance bands and was a founder
member of the famous Jimmy Shand band. At the height of his
career he became almost deaf, but a recent remarkable oper-
ation has restored his hearing and he is now playing as well as
ever.

354
A florid version, using the alternative title, of No. 92. Bill
Hardie's setting is strongly influenced by the master of elab-
oration, J. F. Dickie.

355
Undoubtedly one of the most popular pieces in the fiddler's
'entertainment repertoire'.

357
This tune and Nos. 359, 363, 364 are among the most popular
of the bothy ballad melodies. Bothies are the farm-outhouses
where the young unmarried farmworkers used to live. They
were the incubators of many fine songs about farm life, and the
main accompanying instruments were fiddle and melodeon.

362
Written in 1964 in memory of Campbell Connon, an Aberdeen
solicitor who was a keen member and former chairman of
Aberdeen Strathspey and Reel Society.

365
'Trowie tunes' are the Shetland equivalent of the Hebridean
fairy tunes. Tradition has it that they were heard issuing from
the fairy mounds or from the playing of the 'trows' themselves.